THOMAS COOK
Travellers

MOROCCO

BY
JAMES KEEBLE

Produced by AA Publishing

Written by James Keeble
Original photography by Ian Burgum

Edited, designed and produced by AA Publishing.
Maps © The Automobile Association 1995.

Distributed in the United Kingdom by AA Publishing, Norfolk
House, Priestley Road, Basingstoke, Hampshire RG24 9NY.

A CIP catalogue record for this book is available from the
British Library.

ISBN 0 7495 0957 0

The contents of this publication are believed correct at the time of
printing. Nevertheless, the publishers cannot accept responsibility for
any errors or omissions, or for changes in the details given in this guide
or for the consequences of any reliance on the information provided by
the same. Assessments of attractions, hotels, restaurants and so forth are
based upon the author's own experience and therefore descriptions given
in this guide necessarily contain an element of subjective opinion which
may not reflect the publisher's opinion or dictate a reader's own
experiences on another occasion.
**We have tried to ensure accuracy in this guide, but things do
change and we would be grateful if readers would advise us of any
inaccuracies they may encounter.**

Published by AA Publishing (a trading name of Automobile Association
Developments Limited, whose registered office is Norfolk House,
Priestley Road, Basingstoke, Hampshire RG24 9NY. Registered number
1878835) and the Thomas Cook Group Ltd.

Colour separation: BTB Colour Reproduction, Whitchurch, Hampshire.

Printed by: Edicoes ASA, Oporto, Portugal.

Cover picture: Blue man
Title page: local people, Meknès
Above: waterseller, Rabat

Contents

About this Book

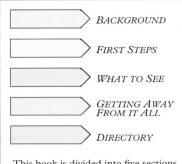

> BACKGROUND
>
> FIRST STEPS
>
> WHAT TO SEE
>
> GETTING AWAY FROM IT ALL
>
> DIRECTORY

This book is divided into five sections, identified by the above colour coding.

Mapping
The maps in this book use internationally recognised country abbreviations:
RIM Mauritania   DZ Algeria   E Spain

Background gives an introduction to Morocco – its history, geography, politics and culture.
First Steps offers practical advice on arriving and getting around.
What to See is an alphabetical listing of places to visit, interspersed with walks and drives.
Getting Away From it All highlights places off the beaten track where it is possible to relax and enjoy peace and quiet.
Finally, the **Directory** provides practical information – from shopping and entertainment to children and sport, including a section on business matters. Special highly illustrated **features** on specific aspects of the country appear throughout the book.

A pilgrim enters the courtyard of the Karaouiyne in Fès, Morocco's holiest mosque

BACKGROUND

*Tunisia is a woman,
Algeria a man, Morocco
a lion.*
ARAB PROVERB

Introduction

*M*orocco is the oldest kingdom in the Muslim world. History is always present here, in the breathtaking architecture of Imperial Cities and of desert kasbahs, and in ancient tombs scattering the hillsides.

The Gateway to Africa, westernmost outpost of Islam, Morocco lies a mere 14km across the straits of Gibraltar from Spain. Despite its close proximity to Europe it is a land still veiled in mystery for most westerners, an exotic kingdom that intrigues and inspires. Here are the sights and smells of Arabia, the legendary souks of Fès and Marrakech overflowing with colourful carpets and pungent spices. Yet here, too, are the rhythms and traditions of Africa, the tribal dances and camel trains of the Sahara, constant reminders of the great continent to the south.

    This is no longer the wild land it was in the days of Barbary pirates and Saharan sheikhs. Tanger is now a rapidly expanding port, destined to be made a 'free trade zone' by the end of the century. Casablanca is a modern business centre of skyscrapers and expressways. Camels have been replaced with Mercedes and motor bikes. And there is even talk of a futuristic bridge or tunnel connecting Morocco and Africa with the continent of Europe. Yet, despite all these developments, Morocco will still surprise, and its subtle blend of ancient mysticism and modern-day capitalism, Arabic conservatism and African *joie-de-vivre* is as alluring as ever. Between two seas, between two continents, Morocco is always dramatic, always unpredictable.

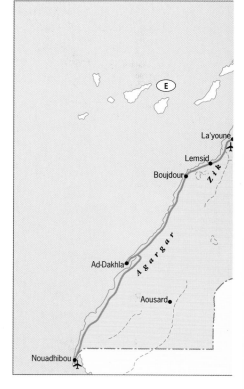

MOROCCO

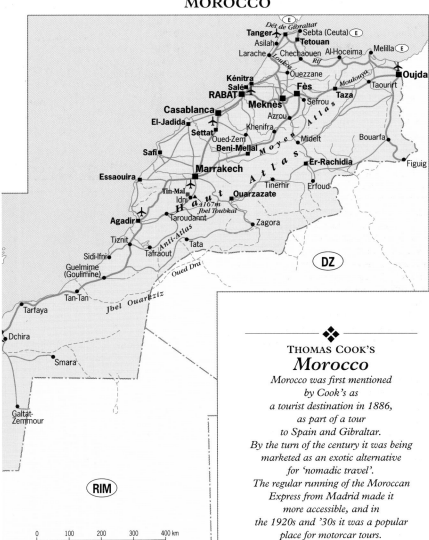

❖

THOMAS COOK'S
Morocco

Morocco was first mentioned
by Cook's as
a tourist destination in 1886,
as part of a tour
to Spain and Gibraltar.
By the turn of the century it was being
marketed as an exotic alternative
for 'nomadic travel'.
The regular running of the Moroccan
Express from Madrid made it
more accessible, and in
the 1920s and '30s it was a popular
place for motorcar tours.

❖

History

10000–5000BC
Neolithic era.

1100–500BC
Trading posts established along the coast by the Phoenicians, merchant sailors originating from presentday Lebanon. Carthage (Tunisia) controls much of North Africa.

146BC–AD250
Carthage falls to Rome. Volubilis, near Meknès, becomes capital of Roman *Mauritania Tingitana*. Roman influence spreads throughout Morocco.

The majestic ruins of the Roman Capitol building at Volubilis, near Meknès

253–683
Roman withdrawal. Morocco divided into Berber fiefdoms. Raids in North Africa by Vandals, then by Byzantines.

683–711
Arab forces invade Morocco. Their leader, Moussa Ibn Nasr, proclaims the land furthest west – 'Maghreb-Al-Aksa' – for Islam. His armies, bolstered by Berber converts, invade Spain in 711.

788–828
Idriss I, exiled from Baghdad after the Sunni-Shiite split in Islam, is welcomed in Volubilis and named ruler by local Berber tribes, establishing the first Arab dynasty – the Idrissids. He is poisoned by followers of the Caliph of Baghdad. His son, Moulay Idriss II, founds Fès.

1062–1145
The Almoravid dynasty emerges from Berber tribes in the south, taking advantage of bickering between Idrissid rulers. Youssef Ben Tachfine conquers as far as Spain. Marrakech is founded.

1147–1248
Ibn Toumert preaches a return to Islamic fundamentalism. His followers conquer territories from Spain to Libya. The Almohad dynasty is formed – a golden age of architecture.

1212
The Almohads are defeated by Spanish Christians at Las Navas de Tolosa.

1248–1465
The Merenid dynasty, originating from southern desert tribes. Proliferation of arts, religious study and architecture.

1465–1554
The Wattasid dynasty assumes power, led by former Merenid advisers. Centralised control wanes. Spain and Portugal establish bases. Religious warrior factions (*marabouts*) control much of rural Morocco.

1492–1550
Spanish seize Granada, ending 700 years of Islamic rule in Andalusia. Influx of Muslim and Jewish refugees.

1554–1669
The Saadian dynasty develops from powerful southern *marabouts*. Spanish and Portuguese driven out. Ahmed el

Mansour conquers Northern Africa as far as Timbuktu.

1609
Bou Regreg pirates pillage from their base at Rabat as far as the Irish coast.

1669
Emergence of the present-day Alaouite dynasty, from Rissani in the south.

1672–1727
Ruthless reign of Moulay Ismaïl, aided by an army of 150,000 African slaves. Foundation of Meknès. British and Spanish evicted from the coast. Ismail attempts to marry the daughter of the French King, Louis XIV, and to convert the British King, James II, to Islam.

1757–1790
Reign of Sidi Mohammed.

1800–80
Civil war in Morocco as the cities of Fès and Marrakech fight for dominance. Power is increasingly devolved to localised Sufi brotherhoods. With the country fragmented and European armies seeking territory in North Africa, Morocco is forced to the negotiating table. Madrid Conference in 1880 establishes European control of Tanger.

1894–1908
Sultan Abd el Aziz leaves bankrupt after high spending, encouraged by European diplomats. French troops land at Casablanca and Oujda.

1912
The Treaty of Fès grants France 'Maroc Utile' ('useful Morocco'), while Spain receives territory on the northern coast and in the Deep South. Tanger is declared an international zone.

1912–56
French colonial governor General Lyautey seeks to preserve traditional architecture and customs. Tanger enjoys an international Jet Set reputation.

1944
Formation of nationalist Istiqlal Party. Demonstrations demanding independence.

1956–57
Independence from France. Mohammed V changes his title from Sultan to King.

1961
Accession of Hassan II.

1975
The Green March: King Hassan II leads 350,000 civilians to claim the Western Sahara from Spain.

1976–88
Polisario rebel fighters seek independent territory in the Western Sahara, supported by Algeria. Morocco's relations with Algeria deteriorate.

1989
Moroccan-Algerian relations restored. Referendum promised on Western Saharan sovereignty. Union of the Maghreb formed between Morocco, Algeria, Tunisia, Libya and Mauritania.

1990–91
Morocco sends 1,300 troops to support the UN in the Gulf War. Pro-Iraqi riots in major cities.

1992
Western Sahara referendum postponed by UN observers after allegations of vote-rigging.

1993
New Moroccan parliament installed in October. Opening of Hassan II Mosque in Casablanca.

Juba II, the Moroccan king who married the daughter of Antony and Cleopatra

IMPERIAL TO COLONIAL

When Moulay Idriss arrived in Morocco in 788 he founded a tradition of imperial rule that has been the cornerstone of Moroccan history. Morocco has been governed almost continuously since then by only seven dynasties.

The Idrissids did not last long. With the death of Idriss II theological bickering among his successors paved the way for a puritanical backlash, provided by the Almoravid dynasty, which swept to power from bases in the southern desert. Rejecting Fès, the Idrissid capital, Youssef Ben Tachfine built the city of Marrakech from which to rule his expanding empire. With Ben Tachfine's death the kingdom fell apart once more, and into the gulf stepped Ibn Toumert, a theologian with a mission to purge Islam of impurity. From his mosque at Tin Mal he spread a fundamentalist message with passionate preaching and the sword. His followers formed the Almohad or Unitarian sect. Toumert's successor Abd el Moumen rode into Fès and Marrakech, effectively becoming sultan of the new Almohad dynasty.

Next came the Merenids, who, having conquered Fès in 1248, started a 200-year passion for building. Occupied with battles in Spain, the Merenid rulers preferred to promote stability in Morocco, allowing the kingdom to become a centre of great learning and culture. In 1492 the Christians retook Spain and the Portuguese captured Atlantic ports, leaving the Merenids empty-handed. Following a power struggle in Fès, a group of viziers saw a chance for a coup and for the next 90 years the Wattasids clung to tenuous power, continually threatened by European raiding parties.

In the mid-16th century, the Saadians from the southern Dra decided it was time to rid Morocco of Christian invaders. They defeated the Portuguese in 1578 but with the death of their leader Ahmed El Mansour in 1603 chaos reigned once more. Time was ripe for a strong leader, and in 1672 the infamous

Ancient mosques, sultans' treasure and colonial intrigue are all part of Morocco's turbulent history

Moulay Ismaïl came to the throne, the first of the present Alaouite dynasty, ruling for 55 years (the longest reign of any Moroccan monarch). Fearsome and brutal, he laid the foundations for a modern Moroccan state, consolidating his kingdom through force and an ambitious building programme. With Morocco well established as a North African power, the 18th and 19th centuries saw growing interest from European superpowers who all wanted a slice of the cake. Unable to withstand such might, Morocco was forced to capitulate, leading to the 1912 Treaty of Fès, which gave France most of the country, with Spain retaining the Atlantic coast. After 1,100 years, imperial rule had become colonial rule.

Fortunately, the French governor proved as wise as any of Morocco's former sultans. Marshal Lyautey was an enlightened general who immersed himself in much of Morocco's history and traditions. Through his influence much of Morocco's heritage was preserved, and its infrastructure greatly improved. Following World War II, Sultan Mohammed V proclaimed independence, supported by the USA and Britain. After much disagreement the French pulled out in 1956 and Mohammed was declared king – the 13th ruler of the Alaouite dynasty. Morocco was an empire once more.

Le Petit Journal

SUPPLEMENT ILLUSTRÉ

FEZ. — UNE AUDIENCE SOLENNELLE DU SULTAN DU MAROC

Geography

'*M*aghreb-Al-Aksa', the land farthest west, lies between the two continents of Europe and Africa. In the north its shores are just 14km from Spain; to the south its borders disappear into the sands of the Sahara desert.

Vital statistics

Morocco is a large country, covering 710,850 sq km since the addition of vast stretches of the Western Sahara (see **History**). Fifteen per cent of this landmass is over 2,000m in altitude, making Morocco one of the most mountainous lands in Africa. Variety is its speciality: there are two coastlines – the Mediterranean, extending for 530km, composed of cliffs and coves, and the 2,800km Atlantic coast, one long beach backed by sand dunes. Its capital, Rabat, has only been an administrative centre since 1912. Like many African countries, Morocco has seen a population explosion this century – from 6 million inhabitants in 1945 to 26 million today, and 40 million predicted by the year 2000. About 75 per cent of this population are under the age of 25.

Landscapes

The north of Morocco seems like a continuation of Europe, with a rocky coast reminiscent of the northern Mediterranean. Further south are three waves of mountains stretching from west to east – the Middle Atlas of high plateaux, inhabited by Berber tribes; the High Atlas, which stretch for 700km and contain 400 peaks over 3000m; and the dry Anti-Atlas, following the borders of the Sahara and marking the topographical beginning of Africa.

To the west are the wide plains of the Oum er Rbia (Mother of Green), and Oued Sebou, Morocco's two greatest rivers. These expanses of fertile land contain most of Morocco's agriculture – olive trees, corn, citrus, sugar cane and vines. East to the Algerian border is a barren steppe region, merging gradually

into the Sahara.

The southern desert is mostly flat and rocky. Sand dunes exist south of the Dra valley and east of the Ziz valley, but otherwise the Moroccan Sahara is *hammada*, stone desert. Oases are common, and provide spectacular bursts of fertility among the rocks and sand.

Climate

Marshal Lyautey, French colonial governor of Morocco, called it 'a cold country with a hot sun'. When it comes to climate, Morocco has a bit of everything. Winter temperatures in the High Atlas plunge to -10°C, and many villages are snow-bound for up to four months. In the Western Sahara it is often above 50°C in places that have not seen rain in over 10 years. Spring and autumn are the best months in the south, but rain storms can cause flash floods in dry river valleys.

In recent years Morocco has been suffering from drought, although rains in 1993 have eased the water shortage. In a country dependent on agriculture, which obtains almost 80 per cent of its electricity from hydro-electric power in the High Atlas, climatic changes can still be a matter of life and death.

Economy

Not blessed with the vast oil reserves of its neighbours Algeria and Libya, Morocco is none the less the largest exporter of phosphate in the world, possessing three-quarters of the world's phosphate reserves. With a decrease in phosphate prices, tourism is rapidly becoming the country's most important industry, with 3.5 million visitors in 1992. Yet 50 per cent of the

work force are still employed in agriculture, representing a quarter of Morocco's economic output.

From countryside to city

While some Moroccans have become wealthy since independence in 1956, and enjoy many of the luxuries considered 'Western', half of the population still work on the land, earning a meagre wage. This disparity between city and country life is a continuing problem: rural depopulation coupled with urban migration has created vast shanty towns or *bidonvilles* in many of the big cities. Casablanca has grown from a small port of 20,000 in 1900 to over 3 million today.

Left: the vast date oases of the Todra Valley
Above right: the kasbah of Tanger
Right: sand dunes of Diabat on the Atlantic coast

Culture

Origins

The indigenous population of Morocco is Berber, a people who originated in ancient Libya. Morocco contains the largest percentage of Berbers in North Africa – 60 per cent of its inhabitants. Yet waves of immigration have left Morocco with a complicated social mix, formed by intermingling communities of Arabs, Berbers, Jews and Harratins.

During the French occupation much was made of the rivalries between Arab and Berber, but today Moroccan society prides itself on being integrated, with most people describing themselves as 'Moroccan'. Although 40 per cent of the population still do not speak Moroccan Arabic as their first language, and 1,000 Berber dialects are currently spoken in scattered village communities, nationalism is a positive force even in the remote countryside. This is a liberal country within the Arab world and differences are respected, beneath the umbrella of the state. Indeed, Moroccans claim proudly that anyone can achieve anything in Morocco; their history is marked with cases of lowly slaves becoming rich sultans.

Morocco's cultural heritage is not only Arab and Berber: the country used to have the largest Jewish population in the Arab world. At independence in 1956 there were 200,000 Jews living in Morocco, but most moved to Israel following the 1967 Arab-Israeli War. More recently, with improved relations in the Middle East, many Moroccan Jews are returning.

Character

Moroccans are a proud people, as befits a race that has controlled the entire Western Mediterranean and produced some of the finest architecture in the Arab world. Like all Mediterraneans they are storytellers, and friendly exaggeration is the order of the day. Getting a straight answer is a skill akin to bargaining. Moroccans enjoy a reputation as the most hospitable of Arab peoples, although the lure of tourist money in the big cities is beginning to override traditional friendliness.

Inshallah

The most common Moroccan saying, '*inshallah*', means 'if God wills'. The Moroccan mentality is directly linked to this philosophy: ultimately Allah knows all and controls all – it is better to sit and wait for his will to happen than to do things yourself. Admittedly things are changing as Morocco seeks to enter the modern business world, but a degree of fatalistic inertia still remains, as it does in many Mediterranean lands (*mañana*, in Spain, is a similar concept).

The influence of Islam is all-

Berber women are highly skilled weavers, following 1,000-year-old traditions

The younger generation of Moroccans are keen to succeed in a fast-developing economy

pervading in Moroccan daily life. Consumption of alcohol in public places is discouraged and in many places men and women do not mix socially outside the home. Yet the younger generation is changing. You will see mothers wearing veils alongside daughters in jeans and make-up. Young couples walk hand in hand, something their parents would never have done. This is a time of great change in Morocco, a transition you will soon sense (see page 24).

Islamic fundamentalism

Far removed from the heartland of Islam, Morocco has always sought to maintain a stable society, allowing all beliefs to be shared. While Islamic fundamentalists struggle for power in neighbouring Algeria, King Hassan II has attempted to combine his role as Imam, leader of the faithful, with a process of economic 'Westernisation'. So far he has succeeded, and it looks unlikely that violent fundamentalism will spill over into Morocco. Yet the spectre looms on the sidelines: during the Gulf War in 1991 pro-Iraqi riots led to numerous deaths and with high unemployment the seeds for religious uprising are there.

Most Moroccans, however, seem content with the secular and religious leadership of their country. They have seen vast improvements over the last decade and have a real sense of patriotism, boosted by Morocco's involvement in the Arab-Israeli peace deal, its selection as the site for the signing of the World GATT deal in April 1994, and its qualification for the 1994 soccer World Cup Finals in America.

MOROCCAN WOMEN

'**A** woman is like an apricot – 18 days and she is out of season.' This Moroccan proverb reveals much about traditional views which state that a woman should serve her husband as long as she is useful to him. Such views are changing in Morocco and today's generation of young women are the first to fight for equal rights in male-dominated areas.

Under traditional Islamic law a man may have four wives, but a woman only one husband. To divorce, a man may say 'I divorce thee' three times (on three separate occasions). In practice, nearly all Moroccan marriages are now monogamous, as women reject their former roles as

Islamic tradition demands that women be covered in public

Times are changing. In Casablanca, Islamic dress codes are challenged by Western fashion

providers of children and servants to men. Or as one Moroccan husband put it – 'it is too expensive these days to keep four wives'.

The veil is dropping. In the streets of big cities you will see women in Western dress, riding motorbikes, going to work. Birth control is now widely available and birth rates have halved. There is now the same number of boys and girls in secondary education. Legally women have many of the rights their mothers only dreamed of (equality in divorce, shared bank accounts and property).

Yet women are still barred from top jobs, and there are only two female members of parliament. The King's wife is rarely seen. City cafés are still male bastions, with women at best confined to back room obscurity. In the countryside life is still hard – women do much of the physical labour, which grants them some economic power but leaves them under male control. Here, girls still leave school at the age of 12 and marry in their teens, to men often 10 years older.

The new generation of Moroccan women has much to do. It is not easy to balance the desire for liberation against the pressure of traditional and respected stereotypes. But Morocco cannot afford to ignore the voice of its women. As King Hassan declared in a recent speech, 'all paths are open to Moroccan women and they must take these paths'.

Politics

Background

One of the world's oldest states, Morocco has a continuous 1,200-year history as a single political entity. Moroccans are proud of their distinctiveness, of their historical empires that stretched across North Africa and into Spain. For much of their history Moroccans have had little say in running their country, controlled by omnipotent sultans. Popular opinion, however, was a great force in obtaining independence, and through Mohammed V and his son Hassan II many steps have been taken to create a democratic infrastructure in Morocco. While it is difficult to transform 'subjects' into 'citizens'

The Parliament building in Rabat, seat of the 353-member legislature

overnight, recent elections in 1993 have led to the creation of a 333-seat parliament.

Government

The 1993 elections, the first for nine years, have sought to devolve power from the palace to a democratically elected parliament. The current 333-seat Moroccan parliament is made up of 222 members elected by public elections in June 1993, and a further 111 members elected by electoral colleges comprising local councils, trade unions and professional organisations in September 1993. All members were elected for six years. The government, headed by a prime minister, is theoretically formed by the majority party in parliament, with the King taking a constitutional role.

In 1993 the traditionalist *Entente* bloc, a four-part centre-right coalition sympathetic to the King, won a 39-seat majority. But in a break from tradition the King, as head of state, asked the minority *Unité* pact, dominated by the Istiqlal and Socialist Union of Popular Forces parties to form a government and to effect what he called 'change and renewal' after 30 years of right-wing rule. This offer was rejected by *Unité*, and a non-party government of technocrats has been agreed under the prime ministership of Mohammed Karim Lamrani, a civil servant who ran the non-partisan elections.

Political issues

Under King Hassan Morocco has entered the world political stage. A leader detached from the wrangling of the Arab heartland, Hassan has been a key mediator in the Arab-Israeli conflict, employing Morocco's close ties with Israel and its Arab status to build confidence on both sides. During the Gulf War Morocco provided troops for the UN force (Saudi Arabia subsequently wrote off a $3 billion loan). Aware that Islamic fundamentalism is growing in neighbouring countries such as Algeria and Egypt, Hassan insists on his Islamic credentials, while attempting to develop his country along Western political lines.

The new government is mandated to move away from centrist state control and to seek the privatisation of 112 companies by 1995. Such policies are likely to endear Morocco to European leaders (but not to advance Morocco's claim for membership of the EC which has been continually rejected).

Hassan's biggest political success to date is the reclamation of vast tracts of the Western Sahara following the 1975

The five-pointed star is the symbol of Morocco

Green March. The war that ensued against Algerian-backed Polisario rebels ended in 1989 with Moroccan promises to hold a referendum on sovereignty. A 2,000km defensive wall, up to 4m high in places, still encloses Morocco's proclaimed territory.

There are, of course, many problems besetting a country seeking to modernise. There is a great disparity in riches, a concentration of wealth and industry in the Rabat-Casablanca area to the detriment of the countryside. The birth rate is still high. Prices for Morocco's main exports of phosphates and sardines have dropped. Islamic fundamentalism, a violent force in neighbouring Algeria, is a shadowy spectre on the fringes of Moroccan politics.

But Moroccans are eternal optimists. They have come far since 1956 and progress continues. One of their great hopes is that tourism will become Morocco's equivalent of crude oil and help to develop the country into a First World nation by the 21st century.

THE ROYAL FAMILY

The 14th ruler of the Alaouite dynasty, King Hassan II claims direct descent from the Prophet Mohammed. He is not only a political figurehead but also 'Ami' al Muminin' – 'Commander of the Faithful', the spiritual leader of Islamic Morocco. That he is revered by his people is unquestionable: every shop, business, home and taxi cab carries his picture and each public appearance is greeted by cheering crowds. This is no forced popularity: he is loved by his people, many of whom believe that without his unifying influence Morocco would not survive.

Ascending the throne in 1961 after the death of his father Mohammed V, King Hassan has sought to combine the traditions of Arabic Morocco with the demands of modern society. In photographs he is the model of a Western politician, in pinstriped suit; at Friday prayers he is always dressed in a white *jellabah*, following strict Islamic custom.

There are a dozen royal palaces throughout Morocco and the King makes sure he visits each region on a regular basis. He, more than anyone, realises the vast variety of his kingdom and the need to provide a focus for its disparate peoples. The new Hassan II Mosque in Casablanca has been criticised as excessively monumental, but it provides a spectacular symbol of Moroccan unity to which everyone has contributed.

Moroccans are proud of their monarch. He is said to possess considerable *Baraka* or saintly power, having survived two assassination attempts in the early 1970s. His 33-year reign has been the most peaceful in Moroccan history and many believe he will continue to lead Morocco into the 21st century. For someone who recently admitted he never thought he would have to be king, Hassan II has enjoyed remarkable political and personal success. But then, as one of his favourite sayings goes: 'It's the style that makes the man.'

King Hassan II

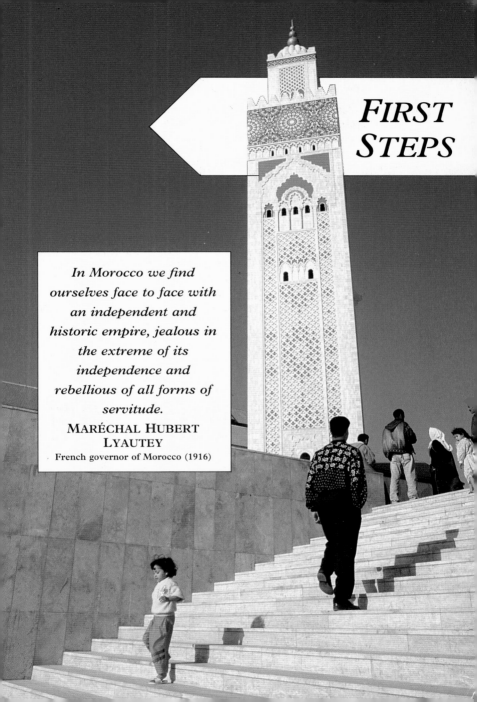

FIRST STEPS

> *In Morocco we find ourselves face to face with an independent and historic empire, jealous in the extreme of its independence and rebellious of all forms of servitude.*
>
> MARÉCHAL HUBERT LYAUTEY
> French governor of Morocco (1916)

Colourful costumes and energetic sales-talk characterise Casablanca's ancient watersellers

BARGAINING POWER

'How much?' is Morocco's number one question. Haggling is a way of life in Morocco, and no visit is complete without attempting to bargain with a merchant in a médina souk. The process is simple. You decide how much you're willing to pay for something. You are quoted an elevated price – commonly three times what it is actually worth. You express incredulity and offer a price 20–30 per cent below what you want to pay. The merchant ridicules your ignorance. So it continues until you agree on a mutually beneficial price.

Centre Artisanals display official fixed prices for crafts in each city. Use these as a guideline for bargaining. In food markets items are fixed price, and attempts at haggling may be seen as insulting. Remember that whatever your economic situation you are perceived by locals as wealthy, and compared with them, in most cases, you are.

CULTURE DIFFERENCES

Many Moroccans, especially in the countryside, are deeply religious. Women who wear veils to preserve themselves from public view are unlikely to appreciate being photographed. Always ask before taking someone's picture. Often you will be asked for money in return: in the case of the colourful snake-charmers and water-sellers of Marrakech this is entirely justifiable – you are paying for a performance as if attending a theatrical performance. However, it is unwise to give money to young children: a child who can earn as much as an adult in a day just from smiling at visitors is unlikely to be pushed to go to school. In some areas 50 per cent of the population is still illiterate, and while literacy rates are improving, paying children for photographs is far from constructive.

THE MOROCCAN SPIRIT

The chaotic, colourful life of Moroccan cities has been fixed for centuries and it is unlikely to become more organised, punctual and subdued overnight. At times it might be necessary to adopt the local philosophy of *inshallah* and go with the flow of things.

While Morocco remains a mysterious country to many outsiders, so the outside world is unknown to many Moroccans, who see foreigners only through imported television shows. Offers of friendship are often genuine and present a fascinating insight into everyday life, but there are always those who see foreigners as little more than walking wallets (see below). Your visit is as much a two-way education as an enjoyable and fascinating holiday.

GUIDES

Official guides are available at all tourist offices and are indispensable – getting round a maze-like medina without them is practically impossible. They are recognisable by their metal 'sheriff's badges' and work on official rates per half and full day. Agree on your itinerary beforehand using the sights described in this book: if you are not interested in shopping, state this firmly – many guides receive large commissions from shopkeepers on tourist purchases and your guide might show undue enthusiasm for getting you into certain boutiques.

Everywhere you go in Morocco, you will be approached by unofficial or *faux* guides. Some claim to be students, but many are just after your money; hardly surprising, in places where one in three men are out of work. Hustlers are best ignored: remain polite, as anger is seen as weakness in the prey. A good way to dispense with unwanted company is not to answer at all. The individual soon gets bored and moves on to fresher pastures. In the event of any trouble find the nearest policeman – hustlers immediately vanish. A sure way to avoid unpleasantness is always to hire an official guide.

It is best to hire an official guide from the local tourist office

ISLAM

Understanding Morocco is impossible without an understanding of Islam. Islam means 'submission', a term which suggests the all-pervading influence of the religion in Moroccan society. Moroccan law is Islamic law; the King is Commander of the Faithful.

Islam was founded by Muhammad, a merchant from Mecca who became Allah's prophet in AD610. 'Allah' is the same God as worshipped by Christians and Jews and for Muslims Jesus Christ is a prophet like Muhammad but not God's son, since God is one, not a Holy Trinity. Islam is unique in denying an

The entrance to the shrine of Moulay Idriss II, founder of Fès

intermediary between God and humankind – there are no priests as such and no liturgy. Prayer is a direct relationship between the faithful and God. The Holy Book, or Koran, was revealed directly from God via the Prophet Muhammad, and combines much of the philosophy of Christianity and Judaism.

Islam is built on five pillars or duties: *chahada*, the profession that 'there is no god but God and Muhammad is the prophet of God', *salat*, prayer five times a day; *zakat*, the giving of alms to the poor; Ramadan, the month-long fast, and *hadj*, the pilgrimage to Mecca.

Sunni, Shiite and Sufi

After Muhammad's death the Islamic world was thrown into confusion. A schism developed between the Umayyad and Abbasid Caliphs, religious leaders chosen to teach the Koran and follow the practice (*sunna*) of Muhammad, and disciples of Ali, Muhammad's son-in-law (*shi'at Ali* – partisans of Ali). This split led to civil war and in the early 8th century many Shiite refugees, facing persecution in Tunisia and Andalusia, flocked to Morocco. Today, however, the vast majority of Moroccan Muslims are orthodox Sunni, like those in the Middle East. In rural areas religion is less orthodox, based on more mystical beliefs surrounding local holymen or saints. Such Islamic mysticism is known as Sufism, and the continuing influence of 'Sufi' brotherhoods, or *Zaiouas*, is felt throughout rural Morocco. Festivals celebrating local Sufi saints are attended by huge crowds (see page 156).

Prayer

In every settlement there is a mosque (*jemma* in Arabic) from which the call to prayer is sung daily by the *muezzin*. Prayers take place at dawn, noon, mid-afternoon, dusk and before sleep. The faithful prostrate themselves towards Mecca, the direction indicated by the mosque prayer niche (*mihrab*). Friday is the Islamic holy day when a congregational prayer is offered at noon (most businesses close by 11.30am). In Morocco entry to nearly all mosques is prohibited to non-Muslims.

Ramadan

The month of Ramadan varies each year, as it follows the ninth month in the lunar calendar when the Koran was revealed to Muhammad. It is always a time of strict fasting, during which the faithful abstain from food, cigarettes and any sexual contact from dawn until dusk. At nightfall the streets erupt, shops and restaurants open their doors and festivities carry on well into the small hours. At sunrise a last meal is taken, the fast recommencing when, as the Koran states, 'one can distinguish a white from a black thread'. The only exemptions from the fast are younger children, pregnant women, the old and sick, and travellers on long journeys. Other Muslims found disobeying the fast are liable to punishment by the authorities. Non-Muslims are free to eat and drink what they like, but moderation from tourists is appreciated. Given the extreme climate in parts of Morocco, especially in summer, the Ramadan fast is a serious undertaking and a time of great introspection.

Moroccan Islam

Morocco has always been different. Morocco's founder, Moulay Idriss, was a Shiite refugee from the Islamic civil war in Baghdad. While today nearly all

Green tiles representing the colour of the Prophet Muhammad on the Grand Mosque in Meknès

Moroccans are orthodox Sunnis, like most Muslims in the Middle East, the remoteness of much of the country's people has led to an interesting blend of Islamic practices and popular spiritualism. Diversity is still the rule, not the exception. *Marabouts*, tombs of the righteous, dot the Moroccan countryside and are revered as places of great power, where women seek fertility, the sick their good health and everyone else good luck. It is unwise for non-Muslims to approach too closely, as these tombs are held in great awe by locals.

LANGUAGE

Moroccans are renowned linguists. French is spoken almost everywhere and many Moroccans are bilingual Arabic-French. In much of the north the second language is Spanish. English is spoken by young people and in major tourist resorts, but in remoter countryside French is essential. Many signposts (all street signs in Fès, for example) are purely in Arabic.

Moroccan Arabic is very different from the classical Arabic spoken in the Middle East. Learning to count would be useful for bargaining purposes and a few common words will always amuse your listeners (see **Practical Guide**, page 183). Berber dialects are also spoken by 40 per cent of the population, in the Rif mountains, the Atlas ranges and the south.

KIF

Kif, hashish and chocolaté, are all terms for cannabis resin, sold in brown cubes or in *majoun* jam. Cultivated in the isolated valleys of the Rif, kif is big business and, as a banned narcotic, illegal. Traditionally, the smoking of kif has been a pastime for Moroccans and tourists alike, but as Moroccan officials state, just the possession of cannabis is enough to incur a three-month to five-year prison sentence. Many dealers also work as informers to the police, and embassies in Rabat carry thick files of foreigners now languishing in Moroccan jails. To be safe, avoid the kif-growing areas in the Rif around Ketama. Picking up hitch-hikers is also ill-advised: if one member of a car is found to possess kif, everyone in the car is arrested.

ITINERARIES

The diversity of Morocco makes it an ideal place for touring. Hiring a car is highly recommended – distances are large, but quickly covered under one's own steam, and you can see much of the country in two weeks. Public transport is plentiful but time-consuming, and for remoter sights, especially in the Haut Atlas (High Atlas), a car is essential. Most international hire companies allow you to pick up a car from one airport and return it to another (see **Practical Guide**, page 180).

The north

A popular summer circuit, the north offers the Atlantic beaches of Asilah and Larache, and the exotic port of Tanger. Families often head to the quiet, unspoilt Mediterranean coastline, while the more adventurous climb to the white towns of Tetouan and Chechaouen and into the wild mountains of the Rif. Many visitors

Setting out from the grandiose city walls of Rabat

combine a week here with a week visiting the imperial cities and the south.

The imperial cities

The four imperial capitals of Morocco provide a fascinating journey from the southern gateway of Marrakech to Fès and Meknès, and across to the majestic Atlantic capital of Rabat. This itinerary includes excursions into the High Atlas, the cedar forests of the Moyen Atlas (Middle Atlas), the ancient Roman city of Volubilis and the Muslim holy town of Moulay-Idriss. Once at the coast, up-market beach resorts such as Mohammedia, Temara and Skhirat offer restful stretches of sand. When planning your trip, remember Marrakech is very hot in summer – spring and early autumn are good times to visit. In winter months the passes of the High Atlas from Marrakech to Fès may sometimes be closed due to bad weather

The south

For many visitors, the south is the highlight of a trip to Morocco. Here, as the High Atlas give way to arid valleys and lush oases, is African Morocco. Camels graze the flat riverbeds of the Dra and Ziz valleys, while at Erfoud, 150m-high sand dunes rise into a blue sky. Dates are the region's main crop – millions of palm trees carpet the otherwise barren landscape. On the coast, Agadir is a modern holiday resort offering excellent leisure facilities. Further north, Essaouira is a more traditional coastal town with a bustling fishing port and enchanting beaches. High season in the south is from September to May, when temperatures regularly exceed 40°C.

Jemaa el Fna is one of the world's greatest street carnivals

SAFETY

Crime rates in Morocco are quite low, but care is advised in big cities where petty theft and pickpocketing are common. Women should be careful when travelling alone – strict restraints on local women, combined with widespread Westernised pornography, mean Moroccan men have a sadly distorted view of the 'availability' of Western females. Morocco has also traditionally attracted many homosexual visitors and in recent years the number of young men offering sex for money has increased – males travelling alone are often assumed to be in Morocco for that sole reason.

In the event of hassle, engage the help of passers-by – shouting '*chouma*' or 'shame' often does the trick. Most Moroccans will come to your aid if they see you are in trouble. If you find yourself with an overpersistent 'guide', head for a policeman – such insistent bothering of tourists is illegal and the tout will soon vanish.

It is now safe to travel to the Western Sahara, following peace accords signed with Polisario rebels. Otherwise, as mentioned, it is best to avoid the remoter areas of the Rif, where kif cultivation is still prevalent.

WHAT TO WEAR

Modest dress is required away from international resorts. Covering of legs and arms is advised for both men and women. Topless sunbathing is rare, mainly confined to the beaches of Agadir. In winter it can get very cold, even in the south when night-time temperatures plunge. The same applies to the High Atlas in summer, where warm clothing is recommended, as nights and early mornings are cold. Contrary to popular belief, it does rain in Morocco, especially in the north (the Rif receives 2,000mm of rain a year) so waterproof clothing is useful in autumn and winter. Sturdy shoes are advisable for the south and boots are necessary for Atlas hiking (see page 136).

WHAT TO SEE

Sit on the rocks, watch the sea,
listen for news...
LOCAL TANGRINO PROVERB

The North

*T*he straits of Gibraltar, the legendary pillars of Hercules, are all that separate northern Morocco from Europe. This wild land of green mountains, towering cliffs and deserted beaches seems a world away from the arid expanses of Morocco to the south. The northern coastline, once inaccessible and underdeveloped, is rapidly becoming one of Morocco's most popular destinations, prized for its clear waters and Mediterranean climate.

Inland, foothills rise to jagged peaks, while whitewashed villages huddle in fertile valleys. In contrast, the great port of Tanger is a growing metropolis offering modern facilities and a cosmopolitan atmosphere. Further east,

NORTHERN MOROCCO

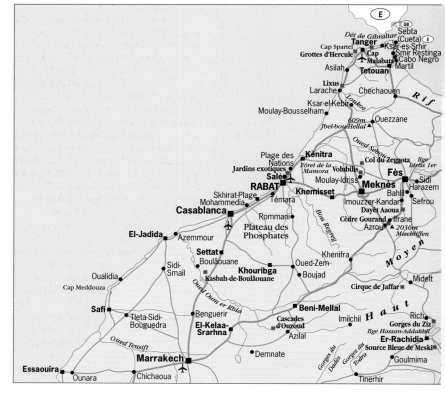

The kaleidoscopic streets of Chechaouen in the foothills of the Rif mountains

Oujda stands on the border with Algeria, a thoroughly Arab city.

The north of Morocco is a region used to visitors. The Phoenicians settled here in 1100BC, followed by the Romans. Moulay Idriss, founder of Morocco, first set foot on Moroccan soil at Tanger in AD788. Later came Portuguese traders, then Muslim and Jewish refugees from the Inquisition in 15th-century Spain. In 1661 the English moved into Tanger, only to be kicked out by Moulay Ismaïl in 1684 (their withdrawal was orchestrated by diarist Samuel Pepys, who admitted a 'loathing' for the port). In 1777 American ships were permitted to dock in Tanger, making Morocco the first country to recognise the new United States.

The north has always been a melting pot for different races, cultures and nationalities. Even today Spain holds two towns along this north coast – the enclaves of Ceuta and Melilla – and Spanish is still spoken in Tetouan and Chechaouen.

Roads are good along the north coast, but bus services are often crowded. It is advisable to stick to main roads when driving in the Rif, the centre of kif production, and not to stop for hitch-hikers or 'accidents.'

Tanger

(Tangier)

*R*omans, Arabs, Portuguese, British, and French have all sought to possess the enigmatic beauty and strategic position of Tanger, the 'queen' of the Mediterranean. Within sight of Europe, washed by Atlantic waves, Tanger was once known as the world's most international city.

The city's history is as turbulent as its seas, continuously swept by tides of Western and Eastern invaders. From the days of Rome to the infamous 'international zone' of this century, Tanger has been a city apart from the rest of Morocco. In its jet-setting heyday, anything went; it was said there was nothing one could not buy in its smoky bars and seedy souks. Artists and writers flocked from America and Europe, drawn to the Bohemian lifestyle.

Today's Tanger is calm – a modern port, with a large tourist trade. Many of the insalubrious night-spots are closed and there are rumours that Tanger is to be made an economic 'free zone', modelled on Hong Kong. Sparkling apartment blocks sprout daily. Further speculation talks of a tunnel or bridge connecting Morocco with Spain in the 21st century.

Guides available from Tourist Office, 29 boulevard Pasteur (tel: 93 82 39).

AVENUE DES FAR
Tanger's main hotel strip, bordering the beach, is a wide avenue also containing numerous beach clubs, once enjoyed by playwrights Tennessee Williams and Joe Orton.

CHARF
At the highest point of the city, to the south of the bay, the disused mosque on Charf Hill offers the best vantage for an uninterrupted view of Tanger.

DETROIT CAFÉ
This restaurant/café was once owned by Brion Gysin, beat poet and friend of The Rolling Stones. In the '60s it was home

The Grand Socco in Tanger

TANGIER

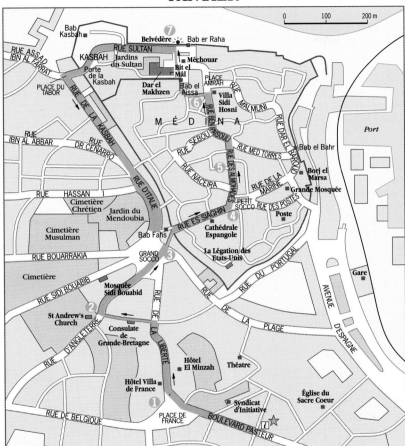

to the hippy set. Today the café is a tourist-pot filled with tour groups. *Rue Sultan (tel: 93 80 80). Open: daily, 9am–7pm.*

GRAND SOCCO (Place 9 Avril 1947)

Not so long ago, warriors from the Rif mountains would ride to the Grand Socco on camels, announcing their arrival with musket shots. Today, the Socco (from souk, meaning 'market') is still lively and Riffians still descend to market on Thursday and Sunday. It was in this square, on 9 April 1947, that Sultan Mohammed first called for Morocco's independence from France.

JARDIN DU MENDOUBIA

Through a large blue door on the western side of the Grand Socco is the Mendoubia Garden, a rambling haven of greenery containing an immense Dragon Tree, said to be over 800 years old. In its trunk one can make out the twisted figure of a man – the captured spirit, so legend has it, of an evil 13th-century Prince.

50 Grand Socco, through the blue gates. Open: daily, 9am–12pm and 3pm–6pm (in theory). Admission free (doorman expects a tip).

KASBAH AND DAR EL MAKHZEN

The kasbah is one of the most famous landmarks of Tanger, a fortress-like settlement overlooking the port. It was in this collection of rambling white houses that Woolworth heiress Barbara Hutton lived, having outbid General Franco of Spain to buy 'Villa Sidi Hosni', the palace where she held extravagant parties for rich and famous guests. Through Bab el Aissa is the Dar el Makhzen, or Royal Palace, built by Moulay Ismaïl to celebrate the British departure from Tanger; it now

The sea gate in the kasbah walls of Tanger

houses an interesting museum. Exhibits include remains from local Roman sites, pottery, rugs and a bone said to come from Jonah's whale. Most pleasant of all are the Andalusian Gardens, aromatic and shady, from where a gate leads to the Belvédère.

Northeast of the Médina, follow rue Ben Raisouli to place Amrah. Kasbah Museum, place de la Kasbah (tel: 93 20 97). Open: daily, except Tuesday, 9am–12.30pm and 3pm–6pm. Admission charge.

LA LÉGATION DES ETATS-UNIS
(American Legation Museum)

Donated to President Munroe by Sultan Moulay Suleiman in 1821, this is the only US national monument outside the United States. The old consulate now houses local works of art, as well as a collection of immaculate antiques. Symbols of Moroccan/American friendship abound; among them a Moroccan rug woven into the stars and stripes, and a 1789 letter from George Washington to the Moroccan Sultan.

8 Zankat America (tel: 93 11 00). Open: daily, 9.30am–12.30am and 3pm–6pm. Admission free.

LA MONTAGNE

When wealthy Europeans first settled in Tanger they built their villas on the wooded Montagne, or mountain, to the west of the port. Now a dense conglomeration of extravagant mansions, it offers a pleasant antidote to the prosaic chaos of the médina: follow directions to the Country Club to view The People's Dispensary for Sick Animals Rest Home, the most curious cemetery in the city.

MÉDINA AND PETIT SOCCO

Smaller than many Moroccan médinas, the Tanger version is as animated and spicy as any (look after cameras and money as you walk). Rue es Siaghin was traditionally the jewellers' street, run by Jewish craftsmen, but now sells a cornucopia of Westernised junk. This leads to the Petit Socco, the heart of the médina and, some would say, of Tanger – a ramshackle huddle of cafés where, in bygone days, you could have bumped into Errol Flynn, Cary Grant and Henri Matisse. Today the clientele has seen better days, but an hour spent in the Café Central will provide many a story.

MUSÉE D'ART MODERNE

Housed in the former British Consulate, this exhibition of modern Moroccan art is both colourful and entertaining. It includes one painting by a former communications minister showing a chaotic tangle of wires, as well as vibrant symbolist work from the Asilah school.
52 rue Angleterre (tel: 93 84 36). Open: daily, except Tuesday, 9am–12pm and 3pm–6pm. Admission charge.

PALAIS MENDOUB (Forbes Museum)

Malcolm Forbes bought this coastal palace in 1970 as a retreat and museum

The American Legation in Tanger

for his vast collection of toy soldiers. *Avenue Mohammed Tazi, Marshan district (tel: 93 56 06). Open: daily, except Thursday, 10am–5pm. Admission free.*

PLACE DE FRANCE

Hub of international Tanger, Place de France once rivalled the Grand and Petit Soccos as a centre of political and literary gossip. Artists, politicians, actors and smugglers mingled daily at the Café de Paris. Opposite, the imposing French Consulate is a reminder of colonial splendour. Next door, the French cultural centre – Galerie Delacroix – holds sporadic exhibitions.
Galerie Delacroix, rue de la Liberté. Open: daily, 9am–12pm and 3pm–6pm. Admission free.

Sunset over the Atlantic and the Cap Spartel lighthouse

TANGER ENVIRONS

CAP MALABATA AND KSAR ES SEGHIR

The long sweep of the bay of Tanger is guarded by two impressive promontories. To the east, Cap Malabata and its 19th-century lighthouse guard the entrance to the Mediterranean, offering views back to Tanger and across to Algeciras in Spain. From the lighthouse rough tracks lead along pine-clad cliffs and down to small, unspoilt beaches. Near by, a ruined folly provides a suitably dramatic counterpoint.

The road east along the coast is little explored by tourists, although it is one of the prettiest in Morocco. About 33km from Tanger, the small resort of Ksar-es-Seghir is a good base from which to explore sandy coves and dramatic cliff paths. Continuing eastwards the road hugs the sea until the Spanish enclave of Ceuta.

CAP SPARTEL AND GROTTES D'HERCULE (Cape Spartel and the Caves of Hercules)

Drive 14km past mansions and umbrella pines west of Tanger and you arrive at Cap Spartel and its lighthouse, a twin of that at Cap Malabata. It is a dramatically beautiful spot – the most northwesterly tip of Africa, where the Atlantic meets the Mediterranean. Across the sea to the north lies **Cabo Trafalgar**, site of Lord Nelson's last battle.

Cap Spartel can be desolate in winter, buffeted by Atlantic storms, but in summer the sun pours down, the sea is turquoise and the beach, stretching 45km southwards to Asilah seems the most beautiful in the world (beware of strong currents – it is not safe to swim).

Just to the south, past Robinson Plage, is one of the most remarkable sights in Morocco: the illustrious Caves of Hercules. Accessible by a series of dank steps, these two caves were once temples of a mysterious prehistoric cult (hundreds of neolithic phalluses were excavated from here in the 1920s). In the international years, bizarrities were order of the day: a party thrown by photographer Cecil Beaton involved one cave being filled with champagne, the other with hashish. The caves' legendary status comes, however, from their seaward entrance, shaped like an inverse map of Africa. In the evening, this natural 'gateway to Africa' provides an unforgettable frame for the setting sun.

Cap Spartel was much prized by the Romans: below the Caves of Hercules lie the jumbled ruins of **Cotta**, an ancient anchovy port, where the furry little fish were skinned, pounded and added to olive oil to make *garum*, a popular Roman snack. Just inland are the ruins of the settlement of Ashaka. In Roman times the area was known as Ampelusium, or Cape of Wine.
Caves of Hercules: open daily, 8.30am–6pm. Admission charge. Cotta and Ashaka are half-heartedly closed to visitors behind a wire fence.

Welcome to Africa – the entrance to the Cave of Hercules, Tanger

---

SPANISH ENCLAVES
When the Spanish pulled out of Morocco in 1956 they retained two northern ports which remain to this day 'Sovereign Territory of Spain'. Ceuta (Sebta in Arabic), the biggest, lies at the northernmost tip of Morocco opposite another enclave, British-held Gibraltar. Ceuta has been heavily fortified since 1580, and there is still a large Spanish military presence. Most visitors come for duty-free shopping – electrical goods, petrol and alcohol – or to catch the ferry. It is a pleasant enough place to wander, especially up to Mont Acho (181m high), offering a good view of Gibraltar. Further east, Melilla is even less interesting: once an export centre for zinc from the Rif, it now relies on duty-free shoppers. Melilla's administration centre is in Malaga, across the sea, and daily flights connect with Spain. Crossing the border into each enclave is a tedious process. Hire cars are not permitted to make the transition.

WRITERS AND ARTISTS

Be it beautiful light, exotic inspiration, inexpensive living or liberal laws concerning drugs and homosexuality – whatever the reason, Morocco can rightly claim to have inspired some of the world's greatest writers and artists.

European artists flocked here at the beginning of the century, seeking to discover the Orient and its exotic secrets. One of the first was French realist Eugène Delacroix, who accompanied a French delegation in 1832. Matisse spent two summers in Tanger, while fauvist Raoul Dufy visited Marrakech. They became quickly addicted to the colours, light and lifestyle: as Matisse exclaimed, 'Tanger, Tanger, I wish I had the courage to get out of here'.

But it was the American writers of the 1940s and '50s who put Morocco firmly on the cultural map. One of the first was Paul Bowles, a young composer from New York who arrived in Tanger with Aaron Copland in 1931 and has yet to leave. Author of *The Sheltering Sky*, in which three Americans travel into the Sahara on a voyage of self-discovery, Bowles was at the centre of a literary pilgrimage which brought the likes of Tennessee Williams, Truman Capote and 'beatnik'

Left: Villa Sidi Hosni, venue for 1920s jet-set parties. Above: Eugène Delacroix and Orson Welles. Below: the tomb of Walter Harris, *Times* correspondent to Morocco

writers Jack Kerouac, Allen Ginsberg and William S Burroughs to Tanger. Burroughs was so fascinated by the city that he used it as his inspiration for Interzone, the nightmarish world described in his novel *The Naked Lunch*. British playwright Joe Orton was a regular visitor until his death in 1967.

Morocco has also attracted film-makers, drawn by guaranteed good weather, low production costs and spectacular settings. Orson Welles filmed much of his *Othello* in Essaouira as early as 1949, and David Lean's *Lawrence of Arabia* was mostly shot near Ouarzazate. So great is Hollywood's interest in Morocco that Ouarzazate now boasts its own film studios, where James Bond films have been made, as well as *Jewel of the Nile* and Scorsese's *Last Temptation of Christ*.

The Northwest Coast

ASILAH

A pretty, whitewashed town on the Atlantic coast, Asilah makes a relaxing change from city bustle. The small streets recall Grecian villages, while wrought iron balconies show a Spanish influence. In August the town hosts an International Festival of Music and Culture, attracting artists from around the world.

This easy-going atmosphere belies a tumultuous past: first a Phoenician fishing port, then Roman Silis, Asilah subsequently attracted the Portuguese, who needed a loading point for gold from Timbuktu. In 1471 they sent an armada of some 500 ships and 30,000 men, who eventually captured the town and constructed sea battlements which survive today.

The **palace of Er Raisuli** (see box) is now an interesting Cultural Centre, with exhibits of local art and works from the International Festival. Three huge gates lead into the médina – the most impressive, **Bab Homar** (down from the palace), still bears the Portuguese coat of arms. In contrast, colourful pop-art murals painted by festival artists adorn many of the whitewashed walls. To the north, the long sandy beach attracts legions of summer tourists.

46km south of Tanger, 232km north of Rabat. Accessible by road or rail (six trains a day to Tanger or Casablanca). Souk: Thursday. Palace of Er Raisuli (tel: 91 70 65). Open: daily, except Friday, 8.30am–12.30pm and 3pm–6.30pm. Admission free.

Whitewashed houses and Portuguese ramparts at Asilah, one of Morocco's prettiest ports

ER RAISULI

Asilah's most infamous resident was a flamboyant bandit named Er Raisuli, who specialised in kidnapping at the turn of the century. President Roosevelt bailed out one of his victims, Greek-American millionaire Perdicaris; *Times* correspondent Walter Harris was chained to a headless corpse in Raisuli's dungeons. Adversaries were often made to walk the plank from his seaside palace. 'Your justice is great, but these rocks are more merciful,' shouted one victim as he jumped. Raisuli subsequently became governor of northern Morocco, until his imprisonment and death in 1925.

Striking murals decorate Asilah's streets

LARACHE

Larache is less visited and more welcoming than Asilah. This was the main port for the Spanish-occupied north until 1956 and Spanish signs still decorate shops and hotels. There is even a small Spanish cathedral. French writer Jean Genet lived here and is buried in the cemetery on the road to Tanger. Today, Larache makes its living from tuna-fishing and meagre tourism.

There are few sights: the large 17th-century Spanish fortress, **Château de la Cigogne** (Stork Castle), offers a fine sea-view (storks nest here from April to September; the ruins are intermittently open – a guide can usually be found), and **place de la Libération** dates from the Spanish era. From this central square a red and white gate leads into the small médina – far from tourist-oriented, and a good place for bargains.

In summer Larache is full of Moroccan tourists enjoying the immense beach to the north, one of the best and safest along this coast.
87km south of Tanger, 191km north of Rabat.

LIXUS

Most foreign tourists to Larache come to see the Roman ruins of Lixus, site of the legendary 'Garden of Hesperides', where Hercules picked golden apples after killing the local dragon (local tangerines are said to be the source of the legend). Founded in 1000BC by the Phoenicians, Lixus was Roman until the 5th century AD, a thriving port dedicated to *garum*, or anchovy paste production. The ruined factories are still visible, along with a theatre/amphitheatre which specialised in wild animal combats. The remains of the baths contain a mosaic depicting Neptune, but most relics were removed to the museum in Tetouan.
5km northeast of Larache, accessible by car, bus or chartered row boat. Open: sunrise to sunset. Admission charge.

MOULAY-BOUSSELHAM

This small beach resort is famous for its lagoon, a reserve specialising in flamingos. To the northeast is Arbaoua hunting reserve, open to lovers of snipe-shooting.
86km south of Larache.

The Rif

*T*he chain of spectacular mountains, stretching 300km to the Algerian border, is traditionally the wildest place in Morocco – the *Bled es Siba*, or 'ungovernable land'. Riffian tribes have always been fiercely independent: prospective conquerors, from Romans to a succession of Moroccan sultans, have consistently failed to gain a foothold in this barren landscape.

Historically the Rif has been the centre of kif production, the Indian hemp grown to extract marijuana. Be cautious, especially around the town of Ketama, the headquarters for this illicit trade: do not stop on the road (ignore hitch-hikers, or apparent 'accidents'), and decline any dubious offers to visit 'farms'.

Times are changing, however. Recently the EU provided a $1 billion aid package to eradicate kif production and provide jobs in tourism. The beautiful Mediterranean coastline is under development, and many of the smaller towns and villages are being 'discovered' for the first time. This region was Spanish until 1956, and the architecture and ambience is Andalusian. Towns like Tetouan, Chechaouen and the eastern border-city of Oujda welcome tourists with traditions and history far removed from those of central and southern Morocco.

AL-HOCEIMA

The biggest resort on the Mediterranean coast, Al-Hoceima enjoys a dramatic setting – a huge bay backed by cliffs, enclosing a magnificent white sand beach. The small fishing village has been overtaken by tourist developments which welcome mainly French package holidaymakers. Three islands lie offshore, all Spanish owned, including **Peñon de Alhuceimas**, an ancient fortress prison.
327km east of Tanger, 293km west of Oujda.

CHECHAOUEN

This exquisite mountain town makes an attractive alternative base to Tetouan. Founded by Muslims and Jews fleeing the 15th-century Inquisition in Andalusia, Chechaouen had been entered by only three Western visitors until the Spanish defeated the great Riffian leader Abd el Krim in 1920 (the illustrious trio comprised a journalist, a cartographer disguised as a Rabbi and a missionary who was poisoned for his trouble). When they finally broke through, Spanish soldiers discovered people speaking Andalusian dialects

Chechaouen's whitewashed walls are said to deter mosquitoes

The valleys of the Rif are rich producers of olives and corn

extinct in Spain for over 400 years.

Today, the town is famous for its houses painted in bright white and blue (rumoured to dispel mosquitoes), and its impressive setting beneath the twin peaks of Jbel Chaouen (Chaouen means 'the horns' in Berber).

Chechaouen's médina is one of the prettiest and most welcoming in Morocco, dazzlingly white in the morning sun and embellished with arches, wrought-iron balconies and delicate stucco. The town is the weaving capital of the region, with 1,500 looms. Wool is brought down from the mountains to be woven into jellabah robes: each village has its own distinctive *jellabah* design, rather like clan kilts in Scotland.

On place Outa El Hammam is the kasbah fortress of **Abd el Krim,** intermittently open to the public. Inside the prisons, where the Berber leader was kept chained by the Spanish, neck, arm and foot irons still cling to the damp walls.

61km south of Tetouan, 118 southeast of Tanger. Souk: Monday and Thursday.

KETAMA
At the heart of the Rif, Ketama was once a popular mountain resort, with tourists coming to ski and hunt on the slopes of neighbouring Jbel Tidiquin, at 2,456m the highest of the Riffian mountains. Today, however, it is more notorious as the capital of kif production, and caution is advised; locals are unlikely to believe you are here for more innocent pleasures.
112km east of Chechaouen, 107km west of Al-Hoceima.

MOUNTS DES BENI SNASSEN (Beni Snassen Mountains)
This fertile eastern limb of the Rif contains two popular and impressive diversions: the large **Grotte du Chameau** (Camel's Cave) – a cavern of spiky stalactites (bring a torch), and the nearby **Beni Gorges du Zegzel** (Zegel Gorge) – a dramatic limestone fault.
90km west of Oujda.

OUEZZANE

This is olive country, a fruit full of *baraka*, or divine blessing, for Moroccans – Ouezzane's 600,000 olive trees produce the finest oil in Morocco. A pretty sprawl of white houses covering the slopes of Jbel-Bou-Hellal, Ouezzane traditionally marked the boundary between the *Bled el Makhzen* and *Bled es Siba*, the governed and lawless lands. It was ruled by Idrissid Shereefs, holy men who claimed ancestry from the Prophet Mohammed. Today the cobbled streets offer glimpses of country life that has changed little over the centuries.

60km southwest of Chechaouen. Souk: Thursday.

OUJDA

Capital of eastern Morocco, Oujda lies in the Angad plain on the border with Algeria. It is surprisingly fertile, with oases and floral avenues nourished by mountain streams. Historically the city has been a military football, passed between marauding armies since the Zenata tribe settled here in the 10th century. Oujda was the only Moroccan city to become Turkish during Ottoman invasions, and was French longer than anywhere else in the country (from 1907, five years before the Protectorate).

There is little to see in town, although the souks are lively and devoid of tourists. **Bab Abd el Ouahab**, or Gate of the Heads, was the exhibition centre for severed enemy heads in the 17th-century. Today it commands a lively square, home to musicians and story-tellers.

For verdant relaxation, try **Lalla Aicha park**, to the east of the médina, or the palm oasis of **Sidi Yahya**, 6km south of Oujda, and its sacred marabouts. Legend states that the tomb of Sidi Yahya is actually that of John the Baptist.

609km southeast of Tanger, 343km northeast of Fès. Souk: Sunday and Wednesday.

SAÏDIA

A developing eastern Mediterranean beach resort, very popular with Moroccans, Saïdia's 15km of sand offers perfect swimming but the crowds are intense in summer.

60km north of Oujda.

The rolling hills of the Rif

Collecting water at Place de l'Oussa in the médina of Tetouan

TETOUAN

'Daughter of Granada', Tetouan was capital of Spanish Morocco until 1956; its art deco buildings are still adorned with Spanish signs and advertising, and many locals still speak fluent Spanish. Tetouan means 'open your eyes' in Berber – wise advice in this intriguing town.

Engage an official guide for the maze of the médina, busy with craftsmen, dyers and tanners. Particularly interesting is **Souk el Houdz**, the Berber market where local women sell red and white striped *foutas*, distinctive Riffian skirts.

From the médina, Bab el Okla (the Queen's gate) leads to the local **Handicrafts School**, located in a converted palace. Do not miss a tour around the classrooms: Tetouan is justly renowned for its woodcraft and pottery mosaics. Just inside the médina walls, the small **Folklore Museum** has older works of art, including displays of marriage ceremonies, a Berber kitchen and Jewish jewellery. To the west of the médina, on place el Jala, the **Archaeological Museum** contains statues and mosaics from Roman Lixus.

57km southeast of Tanger, 281km north of Fès. Official Guide from Tourist Office, 30 avenue Mohammed V. Tel: 96 44 07.

TETOUAN OPENING TIMES
Handicraft School (tel: 96 27 21).
Open: Monday to Friday, 9am–noon and 3pm–6pm. Admission free..
Folklore Museum (tel: 96 69 05).
Open: Monday to Friday, 9am–noon and 3pm–6pm. Admission charge.
Archaeological Museum (tel: 96 71 03). Open: daily, except Tuesday, 8am–3pm. Admission charge..

TETOUAN BEACHES

The nearest beach to Tetouan is **Martil**, a medieval pirate port now backed by modern boulevards and vast apartment blocks. Further north, the long beach at **Cabo Negro** boasts two tourist complexes, including an 18-hole golf course. The 'Black Cape' itself is unspoilt: wild boar still roam its slopes.

Just beyond the small fishing port of M'Diq is **Kabila**, a Spanish-style resort in verdant grounds. The coast's newest development is **MarinaSmir** at Smir Restinga, a glittering marina with restaurants and an aqua-fun park.

Tanger Town Walk

This walk leads through the heart of Tanger and districts made famous by numerous writers and artists, into the colourful maze of the médina and up to the ramparts of the kasbah. For the route, see the Tangier city map on page 33. *Allow 3 hours.*

Begin at the ONMT Tourist office on boulevard Pasteur and continue to place de France.

1 PLACE DE FRANCE

Place de France was the favoured meeting place of writers Paul Bowles and William Burroughs, who used to drink at the Café de Paris. A few doors down is the El Minzah, a luxurious hotel opened in 1931, which served as headquarters for spies and agents during World War II. Today you are more likely to meet Dustin Hoffman in its exclusive bar.

Follow rue de la Liberté 100m from place de France, then turn left, passing the British Consulate on the left, to rue d'Angleterre.

2 ST ANDREW'S CHURCH

St Andrew's has been the focus for the city's English-speaking community since the last century. Its overgrown cemetery is a perfect escape from the hubbub of Tanger's streets. Walter Harris, the *Times* correspondent, is buried here, along with Emily Keane, who married the Shereef of Ouezzane, after he had fallen in love with her as she combed her hair in a hotel window. Open 9.30am–12.30pm and 2.30pm–6.30pm. Churchyard open continuously.
From the church, head between the two lines of palm trees by the bus station to Café Orient and an excellent view over the Grand Socco.

3 GRAND SOCCO

The market in the right-hand corner of the square offers vegetables, fruit, spices (including acclaimed aphrodisiacs) and olives. Further on, the fish market sells everything from shrimps to sharks. Look out for women from the Rif mountains dressed in their distinctive sombrero hats and red and white striped skirts.
Descend rue es Siaghin, on the north side of the Grand Socco, to the Petit Socco. Ignore offers of guides – the route is simple .

4 PETIT SOCCO

This small square enclosed by cafés was once the Roman Forum. In by-gone days it was a place of a million unmentionable deals, and still retains a decrepit charm.
To the left of Café Central take rue des Almohades to place Ouad Ahardane. From here, rue Ben Raisouli leads to the kasbah.

5 THE SOUKS

Wander past displays of leather,

Tanger's Petit Socco has been the scene of a thousand illicit deals

copperware, pottery and carpets – a microcosm of Moroccan crafts. The prices here are likely to be higher than elsewhere in Morocco, but as always it is fun to bargain. Tanger is also renowned for its natural beauty products, including perfume made from goats dung and lipstick derived from mud!
Take rue Ben Raisouli to place Amrah. Just below here is Villa Sidi Hosni.

6 VILLA SIDI HOSNI

Behind these simple white walls was the home of the 'Queen of the Médina', Barbara Woolworth Hutton, who lived here until her death in 1979. Its lavish decorations included 30 gold clocks and a $1 million Indian tapestry encrusted with jewels. Hutton was much loved in Tanger – the mayor even widened the kasbah streets for her Rolls Royce; note the large gateway at place Amrah. Villa Sidi Hosni (closed to the public) is now owned by a Swiss doctor.
From place Amrah pass through Bab el Aissa into the kasbah.

7 THE KASBAH/BELVÉDÈRE

Meaning 'old town', the kasbah has been inhabited since the Middle Ages, although many of the present walls date from Moulay Ismaïl's 18th-century building spree. Place de la Kasbah was the site of public executions up until the 19th century. In the 1960s the site was the gathering place for hippies and musicians from around the world, who congregated at poet Bryon Gysin's Detroit Café (see page 32). From the belvédère there is a memorable view over the Bay of Tanger.
Take rue de la Kasbah through the gateway beneath the Détroit Café and continue ahead to reach Bab Fahs. From here take a taxi back into town.

Central Plains and Moyen Atlas (Middle Atlas)

Central Morocco is the country's most populated region, with 40 per cent of the population living within 20km of the industrialised Atlantic coast. The coastline has seen a dramatic expansion this century: Casablanca alone has grown to 100 times its size in 1900. Industrial complexes, commuter towns and well-heeled beach resorts connect Casablanca, the business capital, to Rabat, the administrative capital.

Inland, the wide plains are rich in phosphates and other minerals, and support the bulk of Morocco's agriculture – fields of corn, olives, fruit and vines (a legacy of former French occupation). Further east, hills unfold from the plains, rising towards Fès and the Middle Atlas. Capital of culture,

often scathing about its prosaic cousins on the coast, Fès is a city of graceful minarets, towering ruins and medieval streets. Neighbouring Meknès was Morocco's capital in the days of omnipotent sultan Moulay Ismaïl, and its gargantuan walls are among the most impressive in the Arab world.

The Middle Atlas region, stretching southwards from Fès, is a wilder land of

The sun sets over the sprawl of Casablanca

CASABLANCA

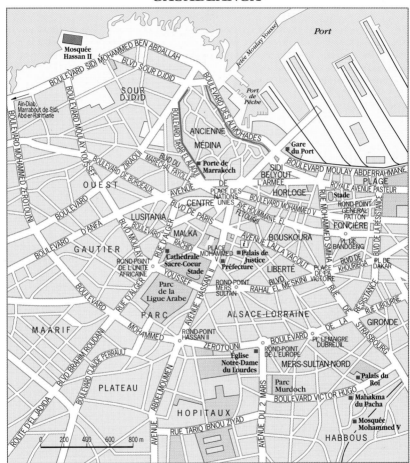

mountains and plateaux. Giant cedar forests cover much of the higher hills, where Morocco's native monkey, the Barbary Ape, roams wild. Snow covers these slopes in winter, and places like Ifrane are more reminiscent of Alpine resorts than African villages. This is the land of the Berbers: low black tents dot the landscape, while herds of sheep and goats roam the valley pastures. Get off the beaten track into the hills and you will be rewarded with waterfalls, lakes and spectacular rock formations that would be at home in any cinema Western.

Casablanca

*T*hose expecting romance and adventure here will be disappointed. Humphrey Bogart never came here, and the film Casablanca was shot entirely in Hollywood. 'Casa' is, in fact, Africa's second largest city after Cairo, with a population estimated at over 3 million (from a mere 20,000 in 1900, before French governor General Lyautey chose it as his administrative capital).

Today, downtown Casablanca is modern, barely distinguishable from Western cities, with wide boulevards, skyscrapers and luxurious hotels – a bustling, hustling business centre. A new twin tower World Trade Centre is planned, providing a high-tech focus for Casablanca's skyline. On the outskirts, shanty-towns or *bidonvilles* present the opposite side of the equation.

Soaring over Casablanca's tower blocks is Morocco's newest landmark, and one of the wonders of modern architecture – the Mosquée Hassan II (Hassan II Mosque). Opened in August 1993, this graceful building on the shores of the Atlantic has finally given Casablanca a symbolic heart. Plans are underway to remodel much of the city, with new avenues leading to the mosque's eight gateways.

To the south, the beach resort of Ain-Diab is Casa's playground: the perfect antidote to the big city.

Casablanca Tourist Office: 55 rue Omar Slaoui (tel: 27 11 77, fax: 20 59 29).

AIN-DIAB – MARABOUT DE SIDI ABD-ER-RAHMANE

A corniche road leads to the Ain-Diab beach clubs, bars and high-class fish restaurants much loved by locals. The clubs all bear exotic names – Tahiti, Lido, Florida – and comprise swimming pools, parasols and restaurants, serenaded by the constant rush of Atlantic rollers. Further on, the long beach of Sidi Abd-er-Rahmane draws enthusiastic soccer players. The *marabout* after which it is named lies at the far end, a mystical tomb on a small island offshore, accessible only at low tide. Sunsets from here are generally impressive.

3km south along the Corniche. Bus 9 from boulevard de Paris .

ANCIENNE MÉDINA (Old Medina)

The Portuguese first settled on this coast in the 15th century. When they returned in the 16th century they named their port

French colonial architecture on Avenue Hassan II

Above: the Marabout of Sidi Abd-er-Rahmane
Right: carpet merchants in the Habbous

Casa Blanca – the white house. This settlement, on a small hill above the bay, was destroyed by the Lisbon earthquake of 1755, and it was not until Arab merchants began to settle in the 19th century that its ruins were cleared and a médina built. Today the médina is sparsely populated and offers little in the way of traditional crafts, although it is a pleasant place to wander. Many of the buildings are marked for demolition to make way for a road to the new mosque.

By the port is a huge shopping centre built in 1988, Centre 2000. .

ANFA

This plush residential district to the west of the centre was once an ancient Phoenician port. It entered modern political history in 1943 when Winston Churchill and President Roosevelt met at the now defunct Anfa Hotel to plan the allied invasion of Sicily and the 1944 D-Day landings.

HABBOUS

When Casablanca became the French administrative capital in 1912, thousands of Moroccans moved to the city

expecting work. In response to the housing shortage created by these immigrants a new médina, Habbous, was built in the 1930s, mimicking traditional Moroccan architecture.

Habbous is a spacious district, an enjoyable place to stroll past shops selling everything from slippers to olives. The buildings, especially the monumental law courts with their emerald roof and massive towers, suggest a hollow film set. Yet for all its artifice, this is perhaps the least frenetic and easy-going of Morocco's médinas. To the east are the walls of the Palais du Roi (Royal Palace).
Boulevard Victor Hugo. Access by bus 5 from boulevard de Paris, or petit taxi.

The colossal entrance gates to Morocco's newest landmark, the Hassan II Mosque

MOSQUÉE HASSAN II (Hassan II Mosque)

Rightly proclaimed as a triumph of faith and craftsmanship, King Hassan's vast mosque on the shores of the Atlantic was finally opened in August 1993 after six years of construction and an estimated 50 million hours worked by 25,000 labourers. It is the second largest mosque in the world, after Mecca, and possesses the tallest minaret (200m high). The mosque's setting, its breathtaking coastal site with Atlantic breakers crashing at its base, was apparently inspired by the koranic verse: 'the throne of God being on the water'.

The mosque's statistics are impressive: 65,000 tonnes of marble were used, 2,500 columns were erected, and 50 Venetian chandeliers were transported from Italy. A laser beam installed in the minaret is visible 50km away. The prayer hall can accommodate 100,000 worshippers – the size of a small airport terminal. And the whole thing cost some $600 million (£400 million), raised almost entirely by public donation. All Moroccans contributed (sometimes not voluntarily) and received certificates, many of which are displayed in homes and shops. Despite outside scepticism (many claim this is King Hassan's projected mausoleum), most Moroccans are proud of their new landmark, exhorting visitors to see it.

Built in white marble, capped with green tiles, the mosque seems a ghostly apparition when viewed from afar, floating above the city. Up close the craftsmanship of the carvings, colourful tiles and cedar roofing is miraculous: many craft traditions, dormant for centuries, were revived during its construction. In the vast *hammam* baths an ancient plastering technique called *tadelakt* was used, mixing black soap, egg yolks and plaster, to prevent humidity. Yet modern science complements tradition: the mosque's roof, covering the huge prayer hall is electronic – on sunny days the faithful pray in the open air; when it rains the roof closes.

Boulevard Sidi Mohammed Ben Abdallah. Access by petit taxi. Open to non-Muslims for guided tours only, Saturday to Thursday, at 9am, 10am and 11am. Tours last for 1 hour. Admission charge. Tour reservations can be made 24 hours in advance by contacting Casablanca Tourism Promotion, Place Zellaka, Avenue des Far Immeuble Helvetia (tel: (02) 44 04 48).

PARC DE LA LIGUE ARAB (Arab League Garden)

Rows of palm trees line this shady park in the centre of the city – a place to sit, sip tea in one of the cafés and admire the rose bushes. At the northern end of the park soar the graceful towers of the Cathédral Sacre-Coeur, once the French cathedral, now closed to the public. Its east wing houses a small medical centre. *South of place Mohammed V.*

PLACE DES NATIONS UNIES (former place Mohammed V)

All major roads to and from Casablanca converge at the hectic place des Nations Unies, just south of the port. The square has been recently renamed, swapping titles with the main administrative square to the southeast.

Here are big hotels, a colonial clocktower, and the constant noise of honking horns and colourful insults. A new avenue leading to the Hassan II Mosque is being built, and when finished will provide a spectacular link from the business centre to the spiritual heart of the city.

PLACE MOHAMMED V (former place des Nations Unies)

This was the colonial core of Casablanca, built by the French in 1920 to house their main administrative buildings. The style they chose was copied throughout Morocco – 'Mauresque', a blend of art deco and Moorish architecture. On the east side of Avenue Hassan II are the gilded columns of the law courts, the French consulate and the *Préfecture*, with its European clocktower. Opposite, the grandiose Post Office looks out onto a wide esplanade dominated by Casablanca's musical fountain, which, if you are lucky, will sing to you and flash lights at night, terrifying the pigeons that inhabit the square.

Parc de la Ligue Arabe, Casablanca

THE MÉDINA

'Médina' simply means 'city', named after the town to which Muhammad fled from Mecca in 622. The médina of Fès is considered to be the most spectacular in the Arab world, a masterpiece of narrow streets and blind alleys enclosed by thick city walls. These maze-like conglomerations provide some of the most memorable sights in Morocco and a chance to witness an ancient way of life at close hand.

The typical médina is made up of several *derbs*, or districts. Traditionally, families of every economic level lived together, the wealthy and notable assuming leadership of the derb. These village-like communities were often proudly independent, rather like the various boroughs of New York or London.

While the complexity of the médina is baffling to outsiders, locals have little difficulty negotiating the chaotic streets. In many places only people born and raised in the médina can become policemen, postmen or guides within the walls. Yet the complexity is not without reason: the narrow streets and tall houses ensure privacy and shelter from the elements. Behind their heavy doors, médina houses are quiet and spacious, organised like mosques, around central courtyards and fountains.

Each *derb* in the médina contains five requisite facilities, providing for all the daily needs of its inhabitants – a mosque, a *hammam*, a bakery, a koranic school and a fountain. Even today you will see children carrying flat bread, or *khobza*, to be baked in the local baker's oven – the oven also heats water for the local *hammam*.

Times are changing for the médinas of Morocco. The wealthy and notable have long since moved to plush residences in the new suburbs. In their place a wave of immigrants has arrived from the countryside, transforming *derb* communities. Many médinas are in a state of dilapidation, with traditional lifestyles disappearing along with historic buildings. The survival of these unique districts is to a large extent dependent on tourism. Do not be daunted – pass through the gateway and help to preserve the heritage of Morocco's medieval past.

The ancient life of
Moroccan medinas
has changed little
in 1,000 years

Fès

*A*ncient capital of the Moorish empire, Fès is the intellectual heart of Morocco and one of its oldest cities, established by Moulay Idriss I in 789 and developed by Idriss II from 809. The world's oldest university lies at its core – the Karaouyine – still considered one of the greatest Islamic schools in the Arab world. Fassis (as inhabitants are known) have always been at the centre of Morocco's cultural and political life, spreading the reputation of their beloved city throughout North Africa and beyond.

Divided into three towns, Fès-el-Bali – 'the old town', founded by Idriss I, Fès-el-Jdid – 'the new town', founded by the Merenids in 1276, and the French-built Ville Nouvelle, the city itself is a unique historical monument. Its médina is medieval, a cauldron for the senses. Passing through its gateways, you are a tolerated alien in a chaotic world that has changed little in over 500 years.

Realising the unique character of Fès, UNESCO began restoring many of its treasures in 1980. Today, the city is re-developing in an attempt to preserve its ancient identity and survive well into the next century.

Fès-el-Bali

Sprawling in the valley, a great sea of houses punctuated by spearing minarets, this is the oldest part of the city, made up of two distinct settlements: the eastern Andalous district, founded by Shiite refugees from Andalusia in 814, and the western Karaouiyne district, founded by Shiite refugees from Tunisian Kairouan in 825. The Andalusians are said to be the best craftsmen, and the most beautiful women. The Karaouiynes are the businessmen, with the money. Even today the two districts are noticeably different: Andalous is calmer, even introverted, Karaouiyne more bustling. Over 250,000 people live in this,

Morocco's largest médina, nicknamed

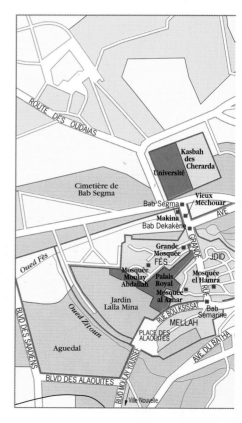

'the most complicated square mile on earth'.

Fès-el-Jdid

'Fès the New' was built by the Merenids in 1276 as a fortress to guard against rebellious Fassis in the old town. A vast administration centre, dominated by the Palais Royal, the town became redundant after the French moved Morocco's capital to Rabat. Today it has a barren feel, enhanced by the empty houses of the Jewish quarter. Most of the city's 17,000 Jews left for Israel following the 1967 Arab-Israeli War.

Ville Nouvelle

The new town comprises the main administrative buildings along avenue Hassan II and the hub of café society and shops on boulevard Mohammed V. *Guides to Fès available from the Tourist Centre, place Mohammed V (tel: 62 47 69).*

FÈS

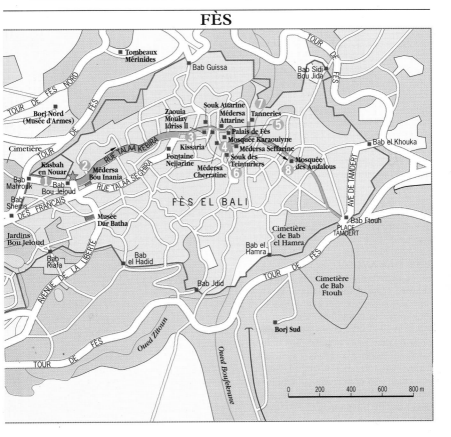

The blue exterior of Bab Boujeloud, the main entrance to the Fès médina

BAB BOU JELOUD

Bab Bou Jeloud is the main entrance to the médina, the traditional gateway to Fès. Its adjacent square has recently been restructured, with buses and taxis moved to a new station outside the walls (see pages 82–3).

BAB DEKAKÈNE

More a castle than a gateway, the 14th-century 'Gate of the Benches', where criminals were once judged, is an impressive entrance into Fès-el-Jdid. Here, in 1437, a Portuguese prince was hung upside down for four days before being stuffed and displayed by the gate for 30 years. Further on, at Bab Seba, workmen still await potential employers, leaning against the wall, tools in hand, as they have for centuries.

Near western end of avenue des Français.

BORJ NORD

Situated on the northern hillside, Borj Nord is a formidable fortress. It was built in the 16th century by Saadian Sultan El Mansour to subdue the Fassis, and offers a panoramic view across the valley; it now houses an arms museum with ornate rifles and a 12-tonne cannon called *Fatima*, used by El Mansour to blow up the Portuguese at the Battle of the Three Kings in 1578.

Borj Nord, by the Hotel Merinides. Access by petit taxi. Open: daily, except Tuesday, 8am–noon and 2.30pm–6pm. Admission charge.

FONDOUKS AND SOUKS

Fès is the capital of handicrafts. Its souks offer the finest, although not necessarily the cheapest Moroccan crafts, and a wander through the teeming streets is unforgettable. Yet this is not a mere tourist attraction: the médina's souks have been here for centuries, a living history that defies the outside world (see page 148).

FONTAINE NEJJARINE
Place Nejjarine lies at the end of the Nejjarine (carpenters') souk, a street filled with the sweet scent of cedarwood. The 18th-century fountain in the square is capped by a finely carved canopy, inlaid with colourful mosaics. At the back of the square, the quarter's *fondouk*, equally well decorated, is undergoing renovation.
20m south of Souk Attarine, 20m west of Zaouia Moulay Idriss II.

JARDINS BOU JELOUD
The gardens have suffered greatly from recent drought, but they are now under renovation by UNESCO. A large water wheel, once used to irrigate the bamboo and exotic flowers, stands to the south.
South of avenue des Français.

KARAOUIYNE MOSQUE
All streets in the médina are said to lead to the Karaouiyne, its spiritual centre. The mosque was founded in 859 by Fatima el Fihri in memory of her Tunisian father, and became the greatest university of the ancient Arab world. In the 10th century Pope Sylvester II studied here, before introducing Arabic mathematics to Europe. Classes are still held in the mosque, but it is above all a religious centre. Non-Muslims are not permitted access; from outside the 270 columns, 24 gates and vast courtyard are just visible through surrounding doorways.
East of Souk Attarine. Closed to non-Muslims.

MÉDERSA ATTARINE
Fès is famous for its médersa, dormitory colleges developed by the Merenid dynasty in the 14th century. Each one housed up to 60 students around a central prayer hall, where classes were held. These ecclesiastical colleges were phased out after the Middle Ages in the rest of the Islamic world, but survived in Fès until the 1960s. Some are still used by Karaouiyne university students.

The Médersa Attarine is one of the finest, built in 1325 – a masterpiece of intricate calligraphy, mosaics and cedar carving. Its arches and pillars seem weightless, supporting galleries of monastic-like cells where students lived two to a room.
West of Souk Attarine, opposite the Karaouiyne.

The Karaouiyne Mosque has been altered by every ruler since its foundation

ISLAMIC ARCHITECTURE

Since AD622, when Muhammad founded the first mosque in Médina, Islamic building has been intimately linked with the Koran, the direct word of God. The mosque (literally 'place of prostration') is oriented towards Mecca, Muhammad's birthplace. This direction is marked by the *mihrab*, a small prayer niche where the *imam*, or spiritual leader, will stand to lead prayer. Hung from the ceiling are candelabra, symbolising Allah, who is the light of the universe. The mosque forecourt, the

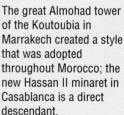

sahn, contains a pool or fountain for ritual ablutions decreed in the Koran. Above the mosque is a minaret, where the call to prayer (*adhan*) is issued five times a day. Moroccan minarets are distinctively square, in contrast to cylindrical versions further east.

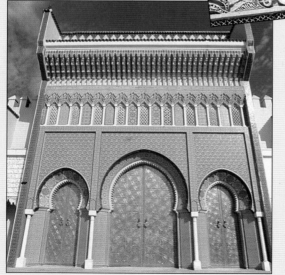

The great Almohad tower of the Koutoubia in Marrakech created a style that was adopted throughout Morocco; the new Hassan II minaret in Casablanca is a direct descendant.

Although Islam forbids iconography, it rejoices in decoration. While Moroccan mosques are usually unadorned, the medersa of Fès, Meknès and Marrakech are intricately ornate. *Zellij* mosaic

Islamic architecture is characterised by its subtle dimensions and intricate calligraphy

them a single verse from the Koran is repeated in angular kufic calligraphy – 'God is great. There is no God but God…'

The keyhole arches and gateways found everywhere in Morocco are also influenced by the Koran. Straight doorways are crowned by an arch representing paradise: Muslims believe that heaven is guarded by seven gateways, through which the faithful must pass.

decorations, delicate calligraphy or 'God's spiders' webs' cover façades and columns. Such art seeks to draw attention from the real world towards a more spiritual one. The repetition of patterns, seemingly endless, seek not to focus the eye but to liberate it, to take it towards paradise. Black and white interlocking patterns often surround the medersa, symbolising the opposite forces of good and evil, while below

Ritual purification at Médersa Bou Inania (above), surrounded by intricately carved partitions (below)

MÉDERSA BOU INANIA

The Médersa Bou Inania is the most
beautiful of all Merenid monuments.
Built on a larger and even more
impressive scale than the Attarine, not a
centimetre of its façades is left
unadorned, the whole building soaring
heavenwards in spiralling decoration. It
was built by Abou Inan, a sultan famous
for committing gruesome murders and
fathering 325 sons. Legend states that he
was criticised by religious elders for
marrying a prostitute in 1355. He
immediately proceeded to build the
Médersa Bou Inania on a garbage dump
and invited the elders to admire his
work. When they expressed amazement
at its sublime beauty he replied: 'As from
garbage comes beauty, so now my wife
has become pure'.

Outside, the famous water clock, also installed by Bou Inan (who wished to have the time of prayer called from his médersa rather than the Karaouiyne), is under restoration. A recently discovered medieval parchment has finally revealed how it worked.

100m from Bab Bou Jeloud on rue Talaa Kebira.

MÉDERSA CHERRATINE

Currently closed for restoration, the Médersa Cherratine is the largest and youngest college in Fès, with a capacity for 240 students, mainly from the Rif, Oujda and Algeria. Built under the Alaouites in 1670, its style is much more utilitarian than the older médersa. Student rooms are constructed around three courtyards, with a series of latrines and washbasins around the fourth courtyard. There are 120 rooms in total, each designed to house two students. The médersa was inhabited as recently as 1950 by theology students from the Karaouiyne mosque.

Southwest corner of the Karaouiyne.

MÉDERSA SEFFARINE

Médersa Seffarine is the oldest médersa in Fès, founded in 1280 and hiding away down a small lane from place Seffarine. Through the studded door, the interior resembles a traditional house more than a school, its arched balcony suggesting intimate family life rather than spiritual retreat.

Place Seffarine.

MÉDERSA SEHRIJ

Isolated in the Andalous district, the Sehrij predates its more illustrious cousins in the Karaouiyne quarter, having been built in 1321. Little visited by tourists, it retains a peaceful and strangely bewitching atmosphere which makes it one of the most underrated sites in the city. The main attraction is a small ablutions pool filled with water, which reflects the crumbling carvings.

20m south of Andalous Mosque.

MELLAH

Each Moroccan city has a *mellah*, or Jewish quarter, witness to Morocco's history of cultural diversity. The Fassi Mellah was the original; the word means 'salt', a reference to the practice of salting the severed heads of enemies – a task given to Jewish inhabitants. The Jewish population was forcibly relocated from the old town by the Merenids in the 14th century. Now empty, the Mellah still retains a veneer of decaying opulence. The Hebrew cemetery, beautifully restored by UNESCO, is a poignant symbol of the past.

South of rue Bou Ksissat. The cemetery is open daily, 8.30am–6pm. Admission free.

MOSQUÉE DES ANDALOUS (Andalous Mosque)

The heart of the Andalous district is dominated by this majestic mosque, constructed in 860 by Miriam, the sister of Fatima, who built the Karaouiyne (see page 59). The mosque was also used as a university with scholars housed in the neighbouring Sebbayin and Sehrij medersa, or colleges (see **Fès Walk**, pages 82–3).

MÉDERSA OPENING TIMES

All the médersa in Fès have similar opening times: daily, except Friday morning, 8.30am–5pm. Admission charge (there is no single ticket covering all médersa).

PALAIS DAR BATHA (MUSÉE DAR BARTHA)

Dar Bartha palace was built in 1873 by Hassan I in a bid to unify the two towns of Fès. His reign was short and the palace was subsequently used by his son Abd el Aziz, the 'playboy of Fès', for wild parties. Under the protectorate, the building became a crafts museum – still one of the finest in Morocco, displaying the traditions behind the goods you see in the médina .

Eight rooms are ranged around a central courtyard. Visitors are required to take a guided tour, but do not be hurried. Begin with the pottery room, full of local ceramics dating back to the 13th century and using the traditional colour of Fès, blue, extracted from cornflower. Fès is also famous for its intricate embroidery, stitched on each side (unlike that of Meknès, which is single-sided).

A further room is dominated by

The coppersmiths of Place Seffarine are among the most skilled of Fès's artisans

colossal Berber rugs, covering whole walls, and cases of sturdy Berber jewellery from the Middle Atlas. Ornate doorways and gigantic locks used to close the médina at night are exhibited next door, including a 1,100-year-old inscription from the Karaouiyne Mosque, and a magnificent 16th-century marble doorway from the El Badi palace in Marrakech.

The pretty Andalusian garden hosts concerts in the summer.

Bou Jeloud/Place de l'Istiqlal, just south of Bab Bou Jeloud. Open: daily, except Tuesday, 9am–noon and 3pm–5.30pm (tel: 634116). Admission charge.

PALAIS ROYAL (Dar el Makhzen)

This vast palace complex is the biggest in Morocco, extended over seven centuries by various Moroccan sultans but unfortunately, like all the royal palaces, closed to visitors. An idea of its extravagant decoration is given by the gateways on place des Alaouites. These seven brass doors, delicately engraved by Fès' finest craftsmen, were commissioned by Hassan II in 1968, and represent the doors to the seven heavens of Islam. The surrounding mosaics symbolise the union of the blue of Fès with the green of the Prophet, while the inscription above the gateways reads 'Welcome. Enter in Peace'. Twice a year the brass is meticulously cleaned with lemon juice.

Place des Alaouites.

PLACE SEFFARINE

This picturesque square is home to the copperworkers of Fès, who hammer at huge couscous pots alongside the ancient fig trees. The square's fountain, trickling from the wall of the Karaouiyne library (one of the most important in the Islamic

world, but closed to visitors), was fashioned by a Portuguese slave in the 18th century: locals were so impressed that he was immediately freed.
Southeast corner of the Karaouiyne Mosque.

QUARTIER MOULAY ABDULLAH
The area around the town's two main mosques is quiet and somewhat reserved. Under the protectorate this was divided from the rest of the town, with bars, restaurants and brothels set up for French soldiers.

TOMBEAUX MÉRINIDES
Perched on the northern hillside, these crumbling ruins are all that remain of an extensive necropolis, built to house the Merenid sultans. From this ghostly setting the view over the valley is superb – a seething mass of houses and fragile minarets (there are said to be 365 mosques in the médina alone).
Next to the Hotel Merinides.

ZAOUIA MOULAY IDRISS II
(Mausoleum of Moulay Idriss)
The shrine of the founder of Fès was forbidden to non-Muslims until French occupation in 1911. Today visitors can walk under the wooden bar designed to

Entrance of the mausoleum of Moulay Idriss II, the second most holy site in Morocco

keep out animals and infidels (it is unwise to photograph the interior – this is the second most holy site in Morocco). Its lavish decoration, including clocks and silverware donated by pilgrims, is matched by the dedicated attention of worshippers who come seeking *baraka*, or saintly blessing.
West of the Karaouiyne. Closed to non-Muslims.

The golden gates of the Palais Royal, Fès

Meknès

*W*hen the Berber Meknassas tribe settled in this fertile valley in the 10th century, they founded a city that was to become the capital of an empire. For 700 years Meknès rested in relative obscurity – a trading post fought over for its rich farmland. In 1672, Moulay Ismaïl, one of Morocco's most powerful sultans, chose Meknès as his home. He proceeded to build a colossal town to rival the court of his contemporary, Louis XIV of France, at Versailles.

Little has happened in Meknès since then. After a brief fling with notoriety during French occupation, Meknès still retains the air of a provincial farming town, albeit one boasting some of the most grandiose sights in Morocco. *Meknès Tourist Office: place Administrative (tel: 52 44 26).*

Bab Mansour, the finest gateway in North Africa

BAB MANSOUR
Proclaimed as the greatest gateway in North Africa, Bab Mansour is the symbol of Moulay Ismaïl's magnificent architectural vision. It is named after its architect, a Christian slave who converted to Islam. Legend has it that on its completion El Mansour was asked by the Sultan if he could do even better. Yes, he replied, and was

MOULAY ISMAÏL (1672–1727)

Moulay Ismaïl is a legendary figure in Morocco. He united the country's warring tribes, defended the kingdom against Turkish invasion, and chased the English and Spanish from the northern coast. Yet he is remembered as much for his spectacular cruelty as for his impressive political achievements.

His first act as Sultan was to dispatch 700 enemy heads to Fès and Marrakech – a warning to prospective rebels. He had 30,000 slaves building Meknès; it was said he would slice off their heads at will and build bridges from the lashed bodies of prisoners.

He had 500 sons and countless daughters (many were strangled at birth), and attempted to marry the daughter of the French King Louis XIV (he was refused). He was protected by a fearsome bodyguard of 25,000 Sudanese slaves, whose descendants guard the present King.

That Moulay Ismaïl is still revered in Morocco may seem surprising. But he was, by all accounts, a deeply religious man. He tried to convert the British King, James II, to Islam. His explanation for his tyrannical behaviour was simple: 'My subjects are rats in a sack. If I do not keep shaking the sack they will bite their way through.'

---

promptly executed. The gate was actually finished by Ismail's son, Moulay Abdullah, whose praises are sung in the inscription around the top. Its monumental style is enhanced by two flanking arcades, supported by marble pillars ransacked from Roman Volubilis (see pages 72–3).
Place el Hedim.

BASSIN DE L'AGDAL (Agdal Basin)

This vast pool – 400m long, 100m wide and 4m deep, fed by 24km of canals from the Middle Atlas – was built by Moulay Ismaïl to provide water for his troops in time of siege. It was enjoyed by his wives (reputedly numbering an amazing 500) who would stroll along its banks. Today it is a popular swimming pool for daring children, and a car wash for their fathers.
South of Dar el Makhzen, next to the municipal campsite and Heri as Souani.

DAR KEBIRA

Dar Kebira, or Imperial City, contained 50 palaces in its 17th-century heyday. At its opening ceremony in 1677, Moulay Ismaïl ritually severed the head of a wolf and stuck it on the gate as a symbol of his power. This entrance on the left past Moulay Ismaïl's mausoleum leads to the ruined complex – there is little to see: a few massive blocks of stone, only hinting at the extravagance of the past. Opposite is the Dar el Makhzen, still a royal residence whose gardens, once playground to the Sultan's harem, are now a royal golf course. From here, 25km of dramatic red walls surround the city, an ample illustration of Moulay Ismaïl's lust for building. These provide a spectacular backdrop for Meknès' autumn *Fantasia* when Berber horsemen simulate past battles, firing muskets with great glee.
Northeast of place Lalla Aouda. Open access. Admission free.

HERI AS SOUANI

From the royal palace and the vast square where foreign ambassadors were received you come to the Heri as Souani, or royal granary. These cavernous storage rooms are remarkably cool in summer – 4m thick walls ensure that the temperature is constantly below 18°C. Grain was poured in from the high windows and ground by huge millstones, turned by three horses. Deep wells provided water directly from the neighbouring Agdal basin. Look out for the 'sun door', taken from the royal palace: its decorations resemble an expanding sun, supposedly inspired by the French 'Sun King', Louis XIV. The elegant arches at the back of the

MEKNÈS

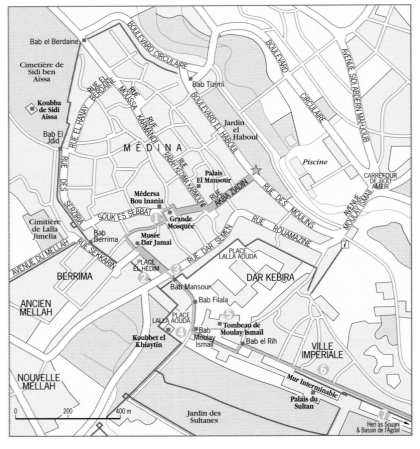

Bab el Berdaine
Cimetière de Sidi ben Aïssa
BOULEVARD CIRCULAIRE
Bab Tizimi
BOULEVARD CIRCULAIRE
AVENUE SIDI ABDERRI MAHJOUB
Koubba de Sidi Aïssa
RUE EL HANAY
RUE EL BERDAINE
RUE MOUSSA KARMANDI
RUE KARMANDI
Jardin el Haboul
Bab El Jdid
MÉDINA
RUE RABAH KEDIMA KARMOUN
Piscine
CARREFOUR DE BOU AMEIR
RUE DES SERTIRA
Palais El Mansour
RUE AKBA ZIADIN
RUE DES MOULINS
AVENUE MOULAY ISMAIL
Cimitière de Lalla Jimelia
Médersa Bou Inania
SOUK ES SEBBAT ❶
Grande Mosquée
RUE ROUAMAZINE
Bab Berrima
Musée Dar Jamai
RUE DAR SEMEN
PLACE LALLA AOUDA
AVENUE DU MELLAH
RUE SEKKARIN
PLACE EL HÉDIM ❸
BERRIMA
❷
DAR KEBIRA
Bab Mansour
ANCIEN MELLAH
Bab Filala
PLACE LALLA AOUDA ❹
❺ Tombeau de Moulay Ismaïl
Koubbet el Khiaytin
Bab Moulay Ismail
Bab el Rih
VILLE IMPÉRIALE
❻
NOUVELLE MELLAH
Mur Interminable
Palais du Sultan
0   200   400 m
Jardin des Sultanes
Heri as Souani & Bassin de l'Agdal

The granaries of Heri as Souani once held supplies to feed an army of 50,000 soldiers

granaries are remains of further store rooms, whose roof collapsed during the 1755 Lisbon earthquake. These are often described by local guides as the Sultan's stables; given that he kept 12,000 horses, this seems a tenuous claim. The real stables are 2km further on, and closed to visitors.

South of the royal palace, next to the Agdal Basin. Open: 9am–noon and 3pm–6.30pm. Admission charge.

KOUBBET EL KHIAYTIN (Prison of Christian Slaves)

This immense underground vault was reputed to be the prison for Moulay Ismaïl's 2,500 Christian slaves, captured by the piratical 'Sallee Rovers' of Rabat (see page 76). It is said that many slaves refused to leave the safety of their dark refuge – during construction of the Imperial City most of them died where they toiled, and their bodies were mixed into the cement of the walls. Wild myths

about the chambers have always kept Meknès' tourist guides in business. One states that three tunnels lead from the chamber to Rabat, Fès and Volubilis. A French tourist did, in fact, disappear down here in 1951, and the tunnels were subsequently blocked up. Scholars now believe the subterranean vaults were nothing more than store rooms.

Above ground, the small domed building was used by Moulay Ismaïl to receive foreign dignitaries.

Place Lalla Aouda. Open: 9am–noon and 3pm–6pm. Admission charge.

Intricate cedar and stucco carving from the Medersa Bou Inania

MÉDERSA BOU INANIA

Many believe this small médersa to be the finest in Morocco, surpassing even its namesake in Fès. It was founded by Abou el Hassan, builder of the Chellah in Rabat, and finished by his son, Abou Inan. Through a narrow hallway opposite the médina's main mosque, the small courtyard, or *sahn*, is a sanctuary from the animation of the streets, its stucco walls adorned with calligraphy. Stairs lead up to a gallery of 13 rooms, occupied by students as recently as 1964 – two students shared a room, reading koranic scriptures by candlelight. From here steps lead to the roof, providing a rare view of the huddle of the médina, across the emerald roofs of the mosque. *Souk es Sebat. Open: daily 9am–noon and 3pm–6.30pm. Admission charge.*

MÉDINA

The médina of Meknès, while not as frenetic nor as ancient as that in Fès, has few tourists and offers a rare glimpse of médina life as it has been led for over a thousand years. It is easy to negotiate and fairly hassle-free. The centre of the médina is dominated by up-market goods – slippers, Western shoes and kaftans. West of here, following the street from the mosque, is Souk Nejjarin, the carpenters' souk. Just to the left is Souk Joutiya as-Zerabi, by a small mosque, where Berber carpets are sold. To the north is a series of chaotic souks, metalworkers and carpenters, all vying for trade. Continue northwest through Bab el Jdid, outside the walls, to the green-roofed Koubba de Sidi Aissa (Marabout of Ben Aissa). Worshippers of this saint, the Aissaoua, are the most fanatical in Morocco. While in trances they are said to pierce themselves with knives, eat live snakes and scorpions and bite heads off chickens. The marabout is closed to non-Muslims and it is unwise to approach too closely.

MUSÉE DAR JAMAI (Dar Jamai Museum)

Built by the same family of viziers (chancellors) as the Palais Jamai in Fès, this 19th-century palace is now one of Morocco's finest museums, set in galleries surrounding a pretty Andalusian garden. On the ground floor are displays of ceramics and jewellery, as well as stunning carpets from the Middle Atlas. Upstairs is the museum's masterpiece: a reconstruction of the vizier's reception room with an immaculate decorative cedar ceiling.

Note also the magnificent silk curtain separating the bedroom on the right. The embroidered cushions are a speciality of Meknès.

Place el Hedim (tel: 53 08 63). Open daily, except Tuesday, 9am–noon and 3pm–6.30pm. Admission charge.

TOMBEAU DE MOULAY ISMAÏL

The last resting place of the flamboyant Moulay Ismaïl is surprisingly subdued. The shrine is open to non-Muslims, but visitors should dress respectfully. Several ante-chambers lead to the main courtyard, where you are required to remove your shoes. Inside, the mausoleum is intricately sculpted, in contrast to Moulay Ismaïl's own epic style. There are four tombs: Moulay Ismaïl lies second from the left, next to his wife and two sons. Behind them stand two grandfather clocks,

Right: carpet-seller and his wares in the médina of Meknès. Below: an austere façade hides the tomb of the flamboyant sultan Moulay Ismail

commiseration presents from the French King Louis XIV in 1700, after he refused Moulay Ismaïl's marital advances towards his daughter. The extensive marble surrounds came from Carrara, in Italy. Salt was bartered in return – 1kg of salt for 1kg of marble.

South of place Lalla Aouda, through Bab Moulay Ismaïl. Open: daily, except Friday morning, 8.30am–12.30pm and 3pm–6.30pm. Admission free.

MEKNÈS ENVIRONS

COL DU ZEGGOTA

About 15km north of Moulay Idriss is the Col du Zeggota, accessible through fields of olives – an ideal place for a picnic, with views over the Meknès plain, the most fertile land in Morocco.

MOULAY IDRISS

White cascades of houses mark Morocco's holiest town, resting place of Moulay Idriss. Non-Muslims are now allowed into the town (until the 1920s infidels would be executed on the spot) but cannot visit the tomb; a 1m-high

wooden bar blocks the entrance. Instead, take the steps to the left, and climb to the Sidi Abdallah el Hajjam terrace (a guide is necessary). From here you can see the green roof of the *zaouia* (tomb) and the arcaded courtyard, where poorer pilgrims sleep. Below, the unique cylindrical minaret of the town's newest mosque, built by a Syrian merchant in 1939, is reminiscent of Middle Eastern architecture. Nearby Donald Duck murals provide an interesting counterpoint.

Moulay Idriss is the site of Morocco's most revered and colourful festival, the moussem of Moulay Idriss, in August or September. A deeply religious occasion, it is open to visitors, but discretion is required.
27km north of Meknès, 47km west of Fès.

VOLUBILIS

Morocco's most important Roman town lies in a remarkable setting in the wide Meknès plain beneath the crags of the Zerhoun mountains.

There was a settlement on this fertile plain during the Neolithic period, but it was Juba II who put Volubilis on the political map in 25BC. A descendant of Hannibal, he married Cleopatra's daughter and introduced Roman civilisation to the town. His son and heir, Ptolemey, was murdered by Caligula in AD40 after which Volubilis came under direct Roman control. The Romans remained here until AD285 when, under pressure from invading Vandals, they withdrew to Rome. For centuries, settlements came and went, until the town was finally deserted in the 18th century. Rediscovered in the last

Green roofs among whitewashed houses mark the sacred Zaouia of Moulay Idriss

century, the Roman ruins were excavated by the French in 1915.

Volubilis is rightly famous for its magnificent *in situ* mosaics. The first of these is found in the House of Orpheus, depicting Orpheus charming the animals with his lyre. Near by, Poseidon rides his sea-horse, while another mosaic contains curious swastika designs – peace symbols brought by Alexander the Great from India.

Most of the visible ruins date from the 3rd century AD. Note the carefully laid street-plan, still visible today – a great contrast to the chaos of Moroccan médinas. In the centre stands the basilica and temple of Jupiter. Near by, small mosaics depict an acrobat jumping backwards off a horse, and fishermen. To the north is the Arc de Triomphe, reconstructed in 1915 from sketches made by Englishman William Boyd in 1726. From here, the Decumanus Maximus, the main street in AD200, extends northeast. Its houses were the most wealthy in Roman Volubilis - stunning mosaics adorn their floors, from the dark red seafood of the House of Ephebus to the seductive portrayals of Diana and her Nymphs in the House of Venus.

Visitors are requested not to pour water on mosaics to enhance their colours – this cracks the stone. *4km northwest of Moulay Idriss. Open: daily, sunrise to sunset. Admission charge.*

MOULAY IDRISS - FOUNDER OF ARABIC MOROCCO

A direct descendant of the prophet Mohammed, Moulay Idriss fled Mecca in 787, following defeat by the Caliph of Baghdad. He landed in Morocco and was welcomed by the community at Volubilis, becoming their imam (spiritual and political leader). A charismatic figure, he soon converted the Berber tribes to Islam and moved their town to a better defended site between two hills – present-day Moulay Idriss. Wary of Moulay Idriss' growing power, the Caliph of Baghdad sent an agent to Morocco in 792, who poisoned the great leader. He was buried in the town of Moulay Idriss, while his son went on to expand the city of Fès.

The unique cylindrical minaret of the Syrian Mosque, built in 1939

Moyen Atlas

(The Middle Atlas)

Giant cedar forests, volcanic mountains, strings of lakes and wind-swept plains grace the Middle Atlas, just 60km south of Fès.

BENI-MELLAL

The largest town in the Middle Atlas with a population of 250,000, Beni-Mellal is a pleasant stopover between Fès and Marrakech. The surrounding plains are an immensely fertile area, producing oranges, olives and sugar cane. The Saturday souk at **Ouled Nenaâ**, 35km southwest, is the biggest and best in the Middle Atlas.

289km southwest of Fès, 194km northeast of Marrakech.

KHENIFRA

Khenifra, in the midst of the Middle Atlas plateau, is a large garrison town with few sights, notable for its strange, dark red buildings and isolated location. Its souks are highly traditional – few tourists venture here.

The S303 north to Aïn-Leuh offers a breathtaking drive through deep gorges and into cedar forests where you will see families of Barbary monkeys (see page 136).

82km south of Azrou, 234km northeast of Marrakech. Souks: Wednesday, Sunday.

MIDELT TO THE ZIZ

South on the P21 to Midelt, the scenery begins to change and the hills become more arid. At the base of the massive Jbel Ayachi range is **Midelt** – the middle of Morocco, famous for its carpets (the most impressive workshop is run by Franciscan nuns – follow signs to Jaffar). West of Midelt is the **Cirque de Jaffar**, a stunning gravel track rising to 3,700m. South of Midelt, just after the inappropriately named village of Rich, you pass through the **Tunnel du Légionnaire**, built by the French Foreign Legion in 1930, and descend into the dramatic **Gorges du Ziz**, a breathtaking canyon of verdant oases.

Midelt 210km south of Fès. Souk: Sunday.

SEFROU AND IFRANE VALLEYS

South of Fès two main roads run into the Middle Atlas. Of these, the **Ifrane Valley** is the most attractive, rising to Immouzer from where tracks lead east to a necklace of small lakes. Further south is **Ifrane**, an apparition of Alpine-style chalets built by French administrators as a ski centre for nearby Mischliffen. This is now one of Morocco's most bourgeois

Palms and rocks form the dramatic landscape of the Ziz Valley gorge

Villages hug the slopes of the barren southern Middle Atlas mountains

resorts – the King has a large palace in the hills.

From Ifrane to Azrou the road offers dramatic views down into the Jaba valley. **Azrou** remains a typical Middle Atlas town, and is a centre for local wood crafts: see the co-operative to the left of the huge rock.

The alternative route south, along the Sefrou Valley, is more desolate. **Sefrou** is an interesting town, with an ancient, well-stocked médina and ochre walls dating from Moulay Ismaïl's day. Its mellah is extensive, although most Jews left in 1967. The town is famous for its cherry festival in June.

Azrou: 60km south of Meknès. Souk: Tuesday. Sefrou: 28km south of Fès. Souk: Thursday.

TAZA

The Taza gap is the only natural pass between the Eastern Rif and the rest of Morocco. The Almohads built defensive walls around Taza in 1135, as well as the impressive **Bab el Rih** (Gate of the Winds). Other sights include Bou Hamra's palace (see box).

To the south, the **Jbel Tazzeka National Park** provides spectacular hiking (see page 140).

TAZA'S MAGICIAN

One of Taza's most infamous sons, Bou Hamra travelled the countryside performing 'miracles' in the 19th century. His star turn involved a conversation with a 'corpse', in which a supposedly dead accomplice was buried in a grave. The man was able to breathe and speak through a thin straw and an amazed crowd heard a 'voice from the dead'. Bou Hamra would then crush the straw with his foot and the accomplice would asphyxiate, to be dug up as a real corpse. The magician met his own end in 1908: he was dragged to Fès, offered to the court lions, who refused to eat him, and subsequently shot.

Rabat

*R*abat is a city of many faces: an old Roman port, an Almohad staging post for the invasion of Spain (*Ribat el Fath*, or 'camp of victory', the origin of its name), a pirate base and, since 1912, the administrative capital of Morocco.

Although a thoroughly Westernised capital, Rabat is proud of its more ancient history: it boasts some of the most impressive imperial monuments in the country. Across the Bou Regreg estuary is Salé, once home to the fearsome 'Sallee Rovers', marauding pirates of the 17th century.
Rabat Tourist Office: 22 avenue d'Alger (tel: 73 05 62).

CHELLAH

Within the Merenid walls of the Chellah are the most hauntingly beautiful ruins in Morocco. Set in a garden of tropical plants are the remains of ancient Roman *Sala Colonia* (closed to the public but visible through gaps in the fence) and the necropolis of the great Merenid leader, El Hassan. The tomb of the mighty 'Black Sultan' lies in a small walled mausoleum, alongside his favourite wife, Shams ed Doura, or 'morning light', an English convert to Islam. Guides will show you round the crumbling halls, pointing out the slender minaret which now houses nests of white storks. To the right of the tombs is a small pool shaded by a banana tree. Here women come to feed eggs to the dark eels that live in its depths – this strange *marabout* is said to grant fertility.
Boulevard Moussa Ibn Noussair. Open: 8.30am–6.30pm. Admission charge.

KASBAH DES OUDAÏAS

Squatting snugly at the mouth of the estuary, the Kasbah des Oudaïas was built by the Almohads in the 12th century. Its main gate, the dramatic Bab Oudaïa, which once housed law courts, now hosts a small commercial art gallery. From here walk along rue Jamaa to the Platforme. Three hundred years ago, the estuary below was filled with pirate ships, which lured schooners onto the sandbanks. Guns from the kasbah would then finish them off. Today you are more likely to see surfers riding the rolling Atlantic waves. Near by is a small carpet workshop, where you will be invited to sit with the women weavers (for a tip).
Rue Tarik al Marsa.

Bab Mrisa at Salé, big enough for pirate ships to sail through in the 17th century

RABAT

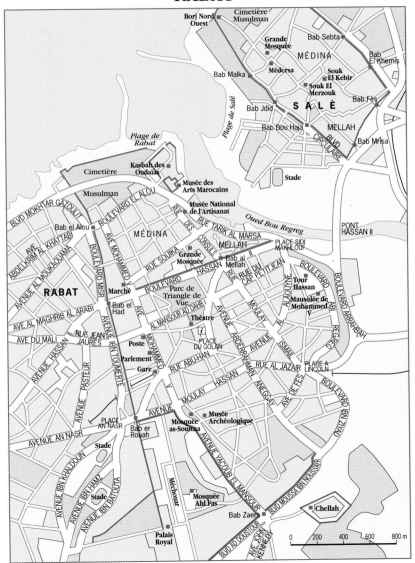

Borj Nord Ouest

Cimetière Musulman

Grande Mosquée

Bab Sebta

MÉDINA

Bab El Khemis

Bab Malka

Médersa

Bab

Souk El Kebir

Souk El Merzouk

Bab Fès

Plage de Salé

Bab Jdid

SALÈ

Bab Bou Haja

MELLAH

Bab Mrisa

Plage de Rabat

Stade

Kasbah des Oudaïas

Cimetière

Musée des Arts Marocains

Musulman

BOULEVARD EL ALOU

Musée National de l'Artisanat

Oued Bou Regreg

PONT HASSAN II

BLVD MOKHTAR GAZOULIT

Bab el Alou

RUE DES CONSULS

RUE TARIK AL MARSA

MÉDINA

MELLAH

PLACE SIDI MAKHLOUF

AVE ABDELKRIM AL KHATTABI

RUE SOUIKA

Grande Mosquée

Bab al Mellah

RUE DU CAP PETIT JEAN

BOULEVARD HASSAN

BOULEVARD

Tour Hassan

AVENUE AL MOUKAOUAMA

AVE MOHAMMED V

BOULEVARD MISR

Parc de Triangle de Vue

Mausolée de Mohammed V

BOULEVARD ARRAHBA

RABAT

Marché

Bab el Had

AVE

AL MANSOUR AD DAHBI

Théâtre

AVENUE ABDERRAHMAN

AVENUE MOULAY AL ISMAIL

Oued BOU REGREG

AVENUE AL MAGHRIB AL ARABI

RUE JEAN JAURÈS

AVENUE IBN TOUMERTE

Poste

MOHAMMED V

PLACE DU GOLAN

AVENUE HASSAN

AVE DU MALI

AVENUE PASTEUR

Parlement

Gare

RUE ABU-HAN

RUE AL JAZAIR

RUE

PLACE A LINCOLN

BOULEVARD IBN ZIAD

AVENUE MOULAY HASSAN

ANEGGAY

AVE DE FÈS

PLACE AN NASR

Bab er Rouah

AVENUE

Mosquée as-Souna

Musée Archéologique

AVENUE AN NASR

AVENUE IBN KHALDOUN

Stade

AVENUE IBN HAMZ

AVENUE YACOUB EL MANSOUR

BLVD MOUSSA IBN NOUSSAIR

Chellah

Stade

Méchouar

AVENUE IBN BATOUTA

Mosquée Ahl Fas

Bab Zaers

BLVD AD DOUSTOUR

Palais Royal

AVE JOHN KENNEDY

0   200   400   600   800 m

Shimmering gold decorates the roof above Mohammed V's tomb

MAUSOLÉE DE MOHAMMED V AND THE TOUR HASSAN

Begun by Yacoub el Mansour in 1195 to celebrate victories in Spain, the Hassan tower is all that remains of the greatest Almohad monument in Morocco. This huge mosque was designed as the biggest in the world, but construction finished on the day of El Mansour's death in 1199. The 50m-high minaret, uncharacteristically placed in the middle of the prayer-hall, was originally supposed to soar 80m; six ramps still lead to its summit, designed to allow the Sultan to ride to the top. Each of the four façades is carved with different designs. The 312 columns at its base once supported an immense roof, destroyed by the Lisbon earthquake of 1755.

Opposite is the white mausoleum of King Hassan's father, Mohammed V, who died in 1961. The dazzling carrara marble tomb was designed by Vietnamese architect Vo Toan, and its interior, a masterpiece of Moroccan craftsmanship, is a fitting resting place for the man who led Morocco to independence. To the side is a smaller sarcophagus containing King Hassan's brother, who died in 1983.

Boulevard Abi Regreg. Open: 8am–8pm. Admission free.

MÉDINA

Rabat's médina is thriving and surprisingly empty of tourists. Rabati carpets are among the best in Morocco, and a whole street is consecrated to them – rue des Consuls, the only street in Rabat where foreign ambassadors were allowed to live in the 19th century. Opposite the médina is a modern handicrafts centre, selling fixed-price alternatives to the médina crafts.

MUSÉE ARCHÉOLGIQUE
(Archaeological Museum)

Tucked away behind the Mosquée as-Sounna, Rabat's archaeology museum contains Morocco's greatest Roman treasures, in particular the *Salle des Bronzes* – an impressive collection of bronze statues from Volubilis, including a 2,000-year-old bust of Juba II, a muscular charioteer, and a lifelike bronze dog, ready to pounce on a Roman postman. In the main hall stands a delicate wooden statue of Juba's son Ptolemy, surrounded by collections of coins, skeletons and Islamic tombstones.

Near Hotel Chellah, Zankat el Brihi (tel: 76 22 31). Open: daily, except Tuesday, 9am–noon and 2.30pm–6.30pm. Admission charge.

MUSEÉ DES ARTS MAROCAINS

Inside the kasbah is Moulay Ismaïl's former palace, now an intriguing Moroccan crafts museum. Moulay Ismaïl greatly favoured Rabat, installing his mercenary guard of Oudaya tribesmen in the kasbah. Today the palatial rooms contain displays of pottery, jewellery and a representation of Fassi and Rabati wedding ceremonies. Flanking the palace gardens are further galleries exhibiting instruments, weapons and colourful clothing.

The Andalusian gardens are exquisite: this is a favourite meeting place for local women, among the fragrant chaos of flowers and citrus trees. Through the gateway overlooking Salé and the estuary is the Café Maure, an institution in Rabat for afternoon tea.

Kasbah des Oudaïas (tel: 73 15 37). Open: daily, except Tuesday, 8.30am–noon and 2.30pm– 6.30pm. Admission charge.

SALÉ

Across the Bou Regreg is Rabat's twin sister, Salé. This was once the more important town, but since 1912 it has been somewhat excluded from the business of the capital. Wander through the ornamental Bab Mrisa, unusually high to allow ships to sail into the town (the channel has long since silted up), to the medina and numerous pottery stalls. At the back of the médina is the Grande Mosquée (Great Mosque) and médersa, built by El Hassan in 1341. The view from the medersa roof across the estuary to Rabat is well worth the detour.

2km east of Rabat. Médersa open: 8am–12 and 2.30pm–6pm. Admission charge.

VILLE NOUVELLE

The French-built new town is the headquarters of Morocco's government, including the parliament building on avenue Mohammed V, and numerous foreign embassies. Just opposite the Parliament, Hotel Balima was Morocco's first European-style hotel (1932) and is still the scene of political intrigue.

Planned as the tallest minaret in the world, the Tour Hassan was abandoned on the sultan's death in 1199

The Atlantic Coast

AZEMMOUR

A small white médina perched on the banks of the Oum er Rbia, Azemmour was once an important fishing port that has now slipped into peaceful obscurity, making it a very pleasant and rewarding excursion from El-Jadida. The terrace around the ramparts of the kasbah offers views back towards Casablanca. Stretching south from the town, Azemmour's long sandy beach is excellent.

16km north of El-Jadida, 96km south of Casablanca. Souk: Tuesday.

EL-JADIDA

It took 40 years for Portuguese warships to capture this strategic port in the 16th century. They stayed a further 200 years until 1769, leaving a style of architecture which is unique in Morocco. The town's sand-coloured médina is laid out in a grid, unlike the irregular streets of Arab médinas. Here the Portuguese Cistern is the main attraction, on the left of the main street – a subterranean reservoir built with elegant arches supported by 25 columns. The tiled floor is lined with lead, which is still impermeable after 480 years – pools of water cast magical reflections of the vaulted arcades. Orson Welles fell in love with the cavernous vault and filmed part of his *Othello* here in 1949. Outside, a gate to the left of the médina entrance leads up to the wide Portuguese battlements and a 10-minute circular walk high above the médina and the Atlantic.

96km south of Casablanca. Portuguese Cistern, rue Mohamed Al Ahchemi Bahbah. Open: 8.30am–noon and 2.30pm–6.30pm. Admission charge.

FORÊT DE LA MAMORA

North of Rabat is a vast forest of eucalyptus and cork oak; note that the bark has been stripped from the oak to make wine corks. Paths criss-cross the forest, which provides an attractive alternative to beach relaxation. Walking and picnicking are its traditional pursuits.

MOHAMMEDIA

A large petroleum port and white sand beach make Mohammedia a somewhat schizophrenic place. Petrochemical refineries mushroom along the shore, but this does not seem to deter up-market holidaymakers from enjoying the chic restaurants, clubs and 18-hole golf course.

28km north of Casablanca.

OUALIDIA

This fishing village is famous for its oysters, which are farmed in the shallow waters created by a series of small offshore islands. The lagoon beach is pretty and the waters here are the safest on the Atlantic coast. A birdwatching paradise, the salt marshes provide excellent breeding grounds for numerous species, including flamingos (see page 135).

76km south of El-Jadida. Souk: Saturday.

RABAT BEACHES

This stretch of Atlantic coastline boasts some of Morocco's most exclusive beaches. South of Rabat, **Temara** and **Skhirat-Plage** are the most popular and up-market, with plenty of restaurants and nightclubs – Temara has a small zoo (open daily 8am–6pm; admission charge), while Skhirat is home to King

Watery shadows beneath the magical vaults of El Jadida's Portuguese cistern

Hassan's summer palace. These are safer waters for swimming than the northern shores of Rabat, but beware – Atlantic currents are treacherous.

North of Rabat is the chic **Plage des Nations**, an awe-inspiring sweep of sand stretching as far as the eye can see. Just before the beach are the **Jardins Exotiques de Sidi Bouknadel** (open 9am–6.30pm; admission charge),

created by a French horticulturist during the 1950s to display plants from Africa and Asia. Two paths can be followed through the Brazilian rainforest, Japanese shrubbery, and into tropical bamboo groves. The place is somewhat dilapidated, but charming nonetheless. *Temara 16km south, Skhirat 26km south. Plage des Nations/Jardins Exotiques 12km north.*

Fès Old Town

This walk takes you into the heart of the médina, a journey back in time through the most colourful souks in Morocco. Begin first thing in the morning. For the route see the Fès town map on pages 56–7. *Allow 4 hours. It is advisable to hire a guide from the Tourist Centre, if only to fend off other 'helpers' (place Mohammed V in the Ville Nouvelle).*

Begin at Bab Bou Jeloud.

1 BAB BOU JELOUD
Built in 1913, this main gateway remains resolutely traditional – a foretaste of the médina itself. Blue-tiled on the outside (the colour of Fès) and green on the inside (the colour of Islam), its archway frames the bustle of the main street, enticing in the uninitiated.
Head straight along rue Talaa Kebira, the main thoroughfare; 80m on your right is Médersa Bou Inania.

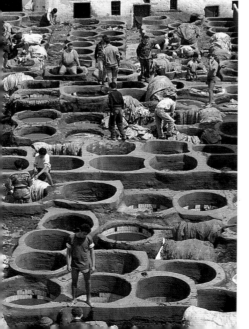

2 MÉDERSA BOU INANIA
The greatest of Fès' médersa, Bou Inania is the only active religious building in the city open to non-Muslims (see page 62).
Continue downhill to Souk Attarine, and the spice stalls and jewellers. Just after the Dar Saada restaurant, turn right.

3 ZAOUIA MOULAY IDRISS II
Five centuries after Moulay Idriss' death, a perfectly preserved body was found on this spot in the centre of Fès' médina. Since then, worshippers have flocked to the site, thronging the ornately decorated *zaouia*. The saint is now patron to many causes, including childless women, and nougat vendors, whose stalls surround his mausoleum (see page 65).
Head east through the Kissaria fabric souk to the Karaouiyne Mosque.

Hives of activity in the midst of the tanneries

The dark green tiles of the Mosquée Karaouiyne are the symbolic colour of Islam

4 MOSQUÉE KARAOUIYNE

When Fatma el Fihri decided to build a mosque in 859 to honour her dead father, she consulted the wisest men of the day as to its location. Once it was chosen, she used only materials dug from this site, to ensure the mosque's purity. Consequently, this is the holiest ground in Morocco (see page 59).

Walking round the north side of the mosque, passing Médersa Attarine on your left, you arrive at a small doorway leading into the cavernous Palais de Fès.

5 PALAIS DE FÈS

This converted 19th-century palace, now a carpet store and restaurant, offers panoramic views from a roof-top café down to the triangular roofs of the Karaouiyne mosque and its huge courtyard.

Walk south to place Seffarine and take the small left-hand street at the end of the square. This leads to the Dyers Souk.

6 SOUK DES TEINTURIERS

Dyers have inhabited this small street since the 10th century. Even today the blackened workshops where pots bubble and fires roar, seem to exist in another age. Traditionally the dyes are natural vegetable colouring, but nowadays chemicals are frequently used.

Head back to place Seffarine. Take rue Méchatine north – a well-trodden path despite its narrowness.

7 TANNERIES

The tanneries are a mesmerising sight – workers dressed only in shorts leap among huge vats, plunging skins into mixtures of dye and pigeon droppings (used to soften the leather). Skins are left for up to two weeks to colour, then dried on surrounding hillsides, as they have since the 16th century.

Return southwards to cross Oued Fès at Pont Bein El Moudoun into the Andalous quarter. Rue Seffrah then rises to the Andalous Mosque.

8 MOSQUÉE DES ANDALOUS (ANDALOUS MOSQUE)

Sister to the Karaouiyne, the Andalous Mosque is famous for its huge carved doorway, built by the Almohads. It is from here, at the highest point of the médina, that the end of Ramadan is announced.

Continue down rue Fekharine to Bab Ftouh. Take a taxi here back to your hotel.

Meknès Old Town

A walk from the medieval médina to the Imperial City of Moulay Ismaïl. For the route see the Meknès town map on page 68. *Allow 3 hours. Avoid noon–3pm, when monuments are closed.*

Begin at the médina gateway on rue Akba Ziadin. Through the arch, after 20m, turn right on to rue Rabah Kedima Karmouni to the kissaria. Turn left, noting the textile boutiques, and continue for 50m until you arrive at the mosque. Follow the walls right and then left onto the médina's main street, Souk es Sebbat. Here are stalls selling fresh mint – Meknès mint is claimed to be the best in Morocco. Another 20m on is the Médersa Bou Inania.

1 MÉDERSA BOU INANIA

A masterpiece of Merenid art, the 'Jewel of the Médina' is impressive for its subtlety. To the right of the ablutions pool is a small prayer hall and *mirhab* facing Mecca, and surrounding the

courtyard are immaculately preserved cedarwood screens, or *moucharabieh* (literally 'see without being seen'), which allowed students a certain privacy. Such screens were also an integral part of harems, behind which wives would languish.

Continue along Souk es Sebbat, past slippermakers' boutiques. After 50m turn left, just after the small mosque. Walk down this crowded street, which skirts the Musée Dar Jamai (see page 67), leading to place el Hédim.

2 PLACE EL HÉDIM

'The square of destruction' is rumoured to be where Moulay Ismaïl carried out many of his executions. It may also be named after the houses destroyed by the sultan to clear an approach road to his palace. The present plaza was remodelled

Zellij tiles decorate the tomb of Moulay Ismail

Ornamental walls of the Royal Palace, where Moulay Ismaïl would drive a chariot pulled by eunuchs

in 1980, and retains little of its former charm. Cafés to the right of the square provide welcome shade and refreshing drinks.
Across the plaza is the entrance to the Imperial City, Bab Mansour.

3 BAB MANSOUR
This monumental gateway escapes few cameras. On the other side are numerous stalls selling freshly squeezed orange-juice and chestnuts.
Continue to place Lalla Aouda.

4 PLACE LALLA AOUDA
Place Lalla Aouda is named after one of Moulay Ismaïl's favourite daughters. It is said she succumbed to eating a peach during Ramadan, and to atone for her sins built a médersa in the médina. To the left of the square are shops selling wool. To the right is the Koubbet el Khiaytin (see page 70).
Head through Bab Moulay Ismaïl.

5 TOMBEAU DE MOULAY ISMAÏL (Mausoleum of Moulay Ismaïl)
The tomb of the tyrannical and much respected Sultan is on the left, just

through the ornamental gateway (see page 70).
Walk on from the mausoleum, through Bab el Rih (Gate of the Winds) to the 'Interminable Wall'.

6 MUR INTERMINABLE (the Interminable Wall)
The 'interminable wall' or 'wall of death', so called because prisoners marched along it to their execution, stretches for 1km between Dar Kebira on the left and the royal palace on the right. It was along this street that Moulay Ismaïl was said to be driven in a chariot pulled by his eunuchs.
At the end of the wall turn right and continue past the palace entrance, through the double gates. Heri as Souani is 50m ahead.

7 HERI AS SOUANI
It is said that 24 pavilions once surmounted the heri, comprising the hidden chambers of the sultan's harem. Today this is the site of a pleasant café. After your visit to the granaries (see page 68) climb here for a deserved drink overlooking the Agdal pool.
Take a taxi from Heri as Souani back into town.

Marrakech and Haut Atlas (High Atlas)

Marrakech gave Morocco its name. It is one of the world's great cities, a place of legend that, despite its popularity as a tourist destination, still manages to remain charged with mystery. The surrounding countryside – the flat plain of Oued Tensift, fed by streams originating in the High Atlas, and the great mountains themselves, towering over the whole of North Africa – provides an unforgettable backdrop to the most sophisticated city in Africa.

The mountains soaring skywards behind Marrakech are named after the giant Atlas, the last of the Titans defeated by the Greek Gods in their battle for the

world. As his punishment Atlas was banished to beyond the western horizon, where he was to hold up the heavens with his shoulders. Legend also states

MARRAKECH AND HIGH ATLAS

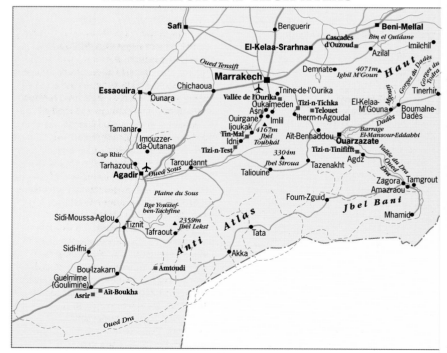

Mount Toubkal and the High Atlas ranges from Ouarzazate

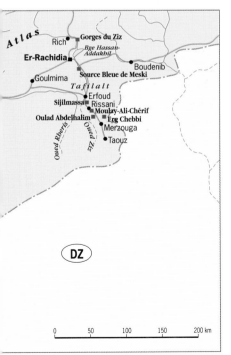

that Perseus came across the giant when returning from slaying the Medusa. When Atlas refused him food and lodging, Perseus turned the truculent giant to stone by showing him the freshly severed head of the Medusa, thus forming the mountains you see today.

The area is still a world apart from the rest of Morocco. The lofty Berber villages clinging to mountainsides seem to have changed little in centuries. Life in regions where snow cuts off valleys for months on end is hard, with a precarious living scraped from sheep farming and meagre cultivation. But the mountain Berbers are among the friendliest and most colourful in Morocco, appreciating and thriving on the stunning beauty of their surroundings. This is a world only recently entered by tourists, and the Moroccan government is keen to preserve its fragile ecology and traditions. Every visitor has a responsibility to do the same.

Marrakech

Marrakech is a city of the south, founded by the Almoravid Berbers of the Western Sahara in 1062. It soon became the capital of their kingdom, and subsequently, under the Almohad king Yacoub el Mansour, the capital of an empire stretching from Spain to Libya and Timbuktu. Under Merenid rule, Fès took over the mantle of royal capital and the rivalry between these two ancient capitals continues to this day.

The walls of Marrakech aflame in the setting sun

Compared with the Arabic elegance of Fès, Marrakech has few monuments. Distinctly African in character, with its dry heat, myriad of palm trees and deep red walls, it is a place to feel rather than see, to experience rather than visit. For many it is the most memorable part of a trip to Morocco.

Marrakech is one of Africa's most luxurious boom towns, with tourism and real-estate development on the increase. Yet the age-old mystery remains. As the sun sets over Jemaa el Fna (see page 90), rhythms and sounds float in the air that have been alive for a thousand years.
Marrakech Tourist Office: place Abdelmoumen Ben Ali (tel: 44 88 89, fax: 44 89 06).

DAR SI SAÏD MUSEUM

This museum was once the palace of Si Said, son of the family that ruled Marrakech at the turn of the century. He was famous for his idiocy, and the family built connecting tunnels from their El Bahia palace to keep an eye on him.

At the end of the museum entrance way is a stone basin dating from 1007, which was brought by Sultan ben Youssef from Cordoba in Spain. Inside are the usual collections of copper and pottery, enhanced by stunning displays of Atlas carpets. The complex dark Azilal rugs are the most impressive, decorated in bizarre geometrical shapes, along with red rugs from Chicaoua. Also of interest are carved fairground swings used at

local *moussem* (festivals) until the 1940s, the display of Berber jewellery, and Berber *burnoose* and woollen boots, strangely reminiscent of Mexican costumes. Upstairs is a replica of a bridal chamber, including the gaudy marriage chair.
East of rue Zitoun el Jdid (tel: 44 24 64). Open: daily, except Tuesday, 9am–noon and 2.30pm–6.30pm. Admission charge.

The bridal chamber in the Dar Si Said Museum

MARRAKECH

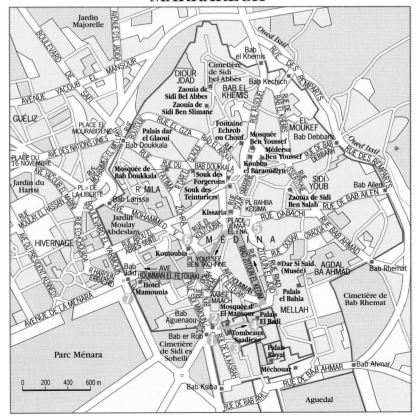

As dusk sets over the Jemaa el Fna, the drums start to beat

GUÉLIZ

Guéliz, Marrakech's French-built new town, is livelier than most. Avenue Mohammed V is full of bars, cafés and restaurants, while the covered market brims with fruit and vegetables.

JEMAA EL FNA

The Jemaa el Fna is the heart of Marrakech, and some would say of Morocco. Nowhere else in North Africa possesses the same hypnotic enchantment, the buzz of thronging crowds, the riot of colour, smell and sound, and the sense of being on the edge of a private ritual. The vast square, ringed by cafés and grill restaurants, is home to the best of Morocco's street entertainers. From mid-morning, when itinerant orange-juice merchants wheel their barrows to surround the square, and acrobats and musicians take their accustomed places, the Jemaa is pure theatre. Monkeys leap, snakes hiss, drums clash and children box. As dusk falls the centre of the square becomes a huge open-air restaurant, with dozens of food stands serving anything from goat's head soup to fried testicles, or simple but delicious *harira*. Tiny gas lights sway, enhancing the ethereal atmosphere. At night the dancers and musicians come into their own, surrounded by small knots of onlookers. The next morning it all begins again.

Paradoxically, Jemaa el Fna means 'assembly of the dead', referring to executions which took place here in the 13th century. Yet the most lively place in Morocco is in no danger of extinction. Giving money to the various entertainers is essential, for they are performing as in any theatre. Snake charmers make their money through charging for photographs, as do the colourful watersellers. Without this money there would be no Jemaa el Fna.
200m east of the Koutoubia.

KOUBBA EL BARAOUDIYN

The only surviving building of Almoravid Marrakech, discovered in 1947, this small domed structure seems inconsequential until you realise it was the prototype for every other edifice in Morocco. Constructed in the early 1100s its keyhole arches, geometric battlements and decorative carvings were the first in

Morocco and are still used today.
South of the Mosquée Ben Youssef. Open:
9am–noon and 2.30pm–6.30pm. Admission
charge.

KOUTOUBIA MINARET

This lone minaret is the spiritual guardian
of Marrakech, overlooking the mortal
chaos of the Jemaa el Fna. Legend decrees
that when it was built it bled its spirit into
the city, which is why all walls and houses
in the médina are the colour of the
Koutoubia. It was begun in 1158 and is
the model for all minarets throughout
Morocco – 1:5 ratio of width to height –
although none surpasses its simple
elegance. It is said the three balls on top
were donated by the wife of Yacoub el
Mansour, who melted down her jewellery
as penance after eating three grapes
during Ramadan.
Southeast end of avenue Mohammed V.

Right: the Koutoubia, model for all Moroccan
minarets. Below: snake charmers, Jemaa el Fna

The oasis luxury of the Jardin Majorelle is a haven from the heat of Marrakech

Hana, the pool of health. It failed to live up to its name, for Sultan Sidi Mohammed in 1873 – his steam boat capsized in the pool, drowning him and his son. A second sultan died here in 1672 – Moulay Rachid forgot to duck under an orange tree and was decapitated as his horse galloped on.

Today the orange groves and olives are the courting grounds for young Marrakechis inspired by the view south to the High Atlas. The buildings across the pool were once a dynamite factory, now under reconstruction for use by the Royal Family.

Rue de Bab Ahmar. Open: sunrise to sunset. Admission free.

Hotel Mamounia

The immaculate gardens of the Hotel Mamounia are easily accessible for the price of a mint tea on the hotel terrace. Originally designed by the Saadiens and embellished by the Alaouites in the 18th century, these beautiful gardens combine European formality with the traditional Moroccan taste for alleyways and flowering shrubs. Winston Churchill and George Bush have strolled these shady lanes.

Hotel Mamounia, avenue Bab Jdid. Tel: 44 89 81.

Majorelle

One of the most visually stunning sights in Morocco is hidden away in a residential quarter to the north of Marrakech. The Jardin Majorelle is a subtropical paradise of bamboo, palms and cactus created by French artist Louis Majorelle. Having fallen into disrepair after the painter's death in 1926, the

MARRAKECH GARDENS

When the dry heat of summer gets too much, there is no better way to seek shade and inertia than heading to one of Marrakech's beautiful gardens. Do as the Marrakechis do: buy a picnic from the covered market on Mohammed V, take a horse and carriage, and find your olive tree.

Aguedal

The Aguedal gardens comprise 3km of olive groves, nourished by a system of underground channels that extends to the Ourika river in the High Atlas. The original gardens were constructed in the 12th century by the Almohads, but the present vista was created in the 19th century by Sultan Abder Rahman, who transformed the park into a working farm. Later rulers built small pavilions or *menzeh* here for their harems. The heart of the gardens is the pool of Sahraj el

gardens were bought by French fashion designer Yves Saint Laurent in 1978, whose villa next door is closed to the public. Fully restored, Majorelle's studio has been converted into an erratically open Islamic art museum. But it is the exterior of the house that catches the eye – painted bright aquamarine, in contrast with the deep foliage, casting magical reflections in the surrounding pools of goldfish. A perfect place to spend a sweltering afternoon.

Avenue Yacoub. Open: daily, except Monday (winter) 8am–noon and 2pm–5pm, (summer) 3pm–7pm. Admission charge.

Parc Ménara

At sunset, when the line of the High Atlas deepens into purple and swallows shriek through the sky, the Ménara gardens must be one of the most gentle places on earth. Once again they are designed around a central pool, founded by the Almohads but redeveloped by Sultan Sidi Mohammed before his untimely end in the Aguedal basin. He constructed the small *menzeh* pavilion that is used in so many publicity shots of Marrakech. The pavilion can be visited, but greater pleasure is found in simply sitting and enjoying the view – the green tiled pavilion set against palm trees and sweep of the giant Toubkal range in the background. This is the favourite picnic ground for Marrakechis, and at weekends and evenings in summer the rows of olives are dotted with family groups feasting off great checked table cloths.

Avenue de la Ménara, southwest of Hotel Mamounia. Open: 8.30am–noon and 2.30pm–6pm. Admission free.

Lengthening shadows on the ornamental Menzeh pavilion of the Parc Ménara

MÉDERSA AND MOSQUÉE BEN YOUSSEF

Originally a Merenid college, the médersa was completely rebuilt by the Saadians in 1564, making it the largest in Morocco. It could hold up to 900 students, and the sense of space is remarkable after the congested colleges of Fès. The Saadians loved decoration and little is left unadorned. The central courtyard is flanked by high teaching rooms leading to the decorative *mihrab*. Next door, the green-roofed mosque is closed to non-Muslims.

East of rue Baroudienne. Open: 8.30am–noon and 2.30pm–6.30pm. Admission charge.

The Saadian Médersa Ben Youssef was designed to house over 900 students

PALAIS DAR EL GLAOUI

Thami el Glaoui was Pasha of Marrakech during the French occupation – thanks in part to French patronage from 1920 until Moroccan Independence. His palace was renowned for its lavish hospitality: the Pasha counted Churchill and Roosevelt among his friends. 'Nothing was impossible', wrote one historian – drugs, champagne, even prostitutes were said to be offered to guests. After his death in 1956 Marrakechis demonstrated their hatred for the Pasha by storming the palace and lynching his supporters (see page 101).

The palace is closed to visitors. There are plans to make it a museum, but while the Pasha is remembered many Marrakechis prefer the gates to remain shut.

Corner of rue de Bab Doukkala and rue Dar el Glaoui.

PALAIS EL BADI

Once the most lavish palace in Africa, El Badi, 'The Incomparable', was built by the great Saadian King Ahmed el Mansour. On its state opening in 1603 the King asked his jester what he thought of his project. 'It will make a fine ruin' replied the fool. One hundred days later the King was dead and the palace looted and destroyed. Moulay Ismaïl spent 12 years stripping it bare of treasures for his own palatial complex in Meknès. There is little left: a huge courtyard, a central pool and four sunken gardens. In the southern corner is a series of caverns, once slaves' quarters and used until this century as a prison. The enormity of the red palace walls and the serene emptiness of the courtyard still impress today. It is not difficult to imagine past luxury, when the palace rooms spread for miles, their walls and ceilings encrusted with gold from Timbuktu.

This is the spectacular setting for the annual Marrakech Folk Festival (see **Festivals,** page 156).

Bab Berrima. Open: 8.30 am–noon and 2.30pm–6pm. Admission charge.

Once the crowning glory of Africa, the El Badi palace is Marrakech's most impressive building

PALAIS DE LA BAHIA

El Bahia, 'The brilliant', was built by Si Ahmed Ben Moussa, brother of Si Dar Said, who started life as a slave and became Grand Vizier in 1894. Approached along a path of palm and orange trees, the palace is centred on a large courtyard, adorned with two fountains marking the Vizier's harem. In the surrounding dark rooms cedar ceilings and a magnificent stained-glass window hint at past elegance. A fireplace was added by French governor Maréchal Lyautey who made El Bahia his residence. From the courtyard a gate leads to a pretty Andalusian garden and shattered pavilions. Only a third of the palace is left: the moment the Vizier died the Sultan's guards stripped the body and the palace, leaving nothing but the great building.

Signposted from rue Zitoun el Jdid. Open: 8.30am–noon and 2.30pm–6pm. Admission charge.

SOUKS

Not as spectacular as the souks of Fès, these cluttered streets do, however, possess an animation and vitality that sets them apart from all others in Morocco. The sights and scents are African – carpets from the southern oasis towns, silver from the pre-Sahara and lizards from the *hamada* vie for attention. Hedgehogs, a country delicacy, grace the stalls of Rhaba Kediam, the apothecaries' square (see page 149).

TOMBEAUX SAADIENS

Having destroyed the neighbouring El Badi palace, Moulay Ismaïl balked at desecrating the connecting tombs of the great Saadien princes. He is said to have seen ghosts as he surveyed the tombs one night, and immediately had the graveyard sealed inside towering walls. The tombs remained hidden until a French aerial survey in 1917 revealed the collection of buildings obscured beneath a jungle of plants. A narrow passageway was built to give access without disturbing the sacred ground. Arrive early – crowds are intense (see page 104).

Place Yacoub el Mansour. Open: 8.30am–noon and 2.30pm–6pm. Admission charge.

Portuguese cannon line the Skala ramparts of Essaouira

MARRAKECH ENVIRONS

LA PALMERAIE

As an introduction to the landscapes of the south, the palm tree oasis of Marrakech takes some beating: 150,000 palm trees, spreading for 10km. The original trees were planted by the Almoravids in the 12th century to provide shade and protection for crops. The ancient underground irrigation canal, or *khettaras*, still survives, fed by water from the Ourika Valley (see page 106).

Today, La Palmeraie is the centre of Marrakech's real-estate boom, with hundreds of low-rise apartment complexes, swimming pools and tennis courts replacing the venerable palm trees. A vast new hotel resort – Les Jardins de la Palmeraie – now commands the northern fringes: where camels once grazed, businessmen now thwack golf balls and the youth of Marrakech go ten-pin bowling in Morocco's first and only bowling alley.

Take 'circuit de la Palmeraie' east from the P7 Route de Casablanca.

RAMPARTS

Marrakech is encircled by 16km of ochre walls, built by Almoravid Sultan Ali Ben Youssef in 1126. Nine metres high, crowned with 200 towers and pierced by nine gates, these ramparts are made of *pisé* – packed clay baked by the sun. The most enjoyable tour around the ramparts is by horse and carriage, hired to the west of the Jemaa el Fna. Prices are reasonable but agree your fare beforehand. Ask to stop at **Bab Khemis** for its lively souk, and the tanneries at **Bab Debbarh**. Here the skins of sheep and goats are soaked in chalk to separate them from their owners, then left to soften for two weeks in pigeon's excrement (hence the stench). Once washed they are soaked in a solution of oak bark and corn and then washed one last time in Mimosa scented baths. The skins are sold at the leather market held here each Friday. For those less enamoured with dead skins, **Bab Doukkala**, to the west, now houses a modern commercial art gallery (open: daily, 9am–6pm; admission free). End the tour with a picnic in the Aguedal or Ménara gardens (see pages 92–3).

THE ATLANTIC COAST

ESSAOUIRA

The most relaxed of all Moroccan towns, Essaouira is a magical place of whitewashed streets, wide sand beaches and a chaotic fishing port, famous for its craftsmen, who work with local thuya wood. In recent years it has attracted artists and photographers, as well as windsurfers who consider Essaouira's surf the best in Africa.

Souirah means 'beautifully drawn', and the town has an incongruous European regularity, designed by a French slave of Sultan Sidi Mohammed in 1760. In Roman times, the offshore 'purple' islands of Mogador (the ancient name for Essaouira) provided shellfish dye for royal cloaks. Ptolemy wore such a cloak to meet Caligula and was murdered for his sartorial superiority (see page 73).

The animated fishing port is the focus of the town. Tourism rivals sardines as the major industry, yet there are few specific sights: the Skala ramparts offer views over the bay and there is a small Sidi Mohammed arts museum (rue Derb Laalouj. Open: 9am–noon, 2.30pm–6pm; admission charge). Visitors spend most time in the woodcraft souks, marvelling at the designs on offer.

South of the port are the sand dunes of Diabat, once a hippy colony led by guitarist Jimi Hendrix. The beach is now home to obsessive windsurfers.
176km due west of Marrakech.

SAFI

A large industrial port, Safi offers a lack of tourists and impressive Portuguese battlements. The Château de la Mer fortress is a ghostly castle (open: 8am–noon, 2pm–5pm; admission charge), and in the médina an old Portuguese chapel recalls a colonial past. Safi's souks are famous for pottery, but modern industry is centred on sardine-packing and phosphate plants to the south. The best beaches are 20km north of the town.
157km northwest of Marrakech.

Trawlers prepare for sea in the port of Essaouira

Haut Atlas (High Atlas)

ASNI AND IMLIL

South from Marrakech the S501 begins to climb at Tahanoute, ascending through the gorge of Moulay Brahim until it arrives at Asni, a one-street town that is the administrative centre of the northern High Atlas. There is nothing to see here, just a row of ragged shops, but it is the hub of the region's public transport and provides accommodation and food for hikers. Imlil is a further 17km south along a tarmac and then a dirt road. The change in scenery is dramatic, climbing 600m along the banks of the Oued Reraïa. Here the valley floor is surprisingly fertile, patchworked with terraced fields where cattle graze. Above it loom the rocky crags of North Africa's highest mountains. Imlil is the main base for trekking in Toubkal National Park, a pretty village, backed by chestnut woods and set beneath a circle of mountains (see page 108).

Asni: 47km south of Marrakech. Imlil: 17km south of Asni.

AZILAL AND CASCADES D'OUZOUD

Less visited than the Toubkal massif, the Azilal range offers some of the finest walking and most dramatic scenery in the High Atlas. Azilal is the administrative centre, an uninteresting garrison town. South of Azilal tracks lead to the Bou Goumez valley and Agouti – the starting point for ascents of 4,071m **Ighil M'Goun**. To the northeast the huge 3,800-hectare reservoir of **Bin el Ouidane** provides much of Morocco's hydro-electric power (drought has led to a marked shrinking of the lake). Fishing, boating swimming and even windsurfing are possible from the village of Bin-el-Ouidane.

The most famous sight in the region is the Cascades d'Ouzoud, northwest of Azilal. These 100m-high waterfalls plunge into a series of deep pools, one of which is popular with swimmers. Surrounding vegetation gives the site a vaguely tropical air. In recent years drought has affected the flow of the falls,

Fruit and donkeys are the specialities of the market at Asni

Oukaïmeden and the snows of the High Atlas

but the location is still impressive. A huddle of hotels and cafés provides a relaxing base.

Azilal: 165km east of Marrakech.
Cascades d'Ouzoud: 26km west of Azilal.

DEMNATE

The *pisé* kasbah of Demnate is one of the few southern kasbahs still inhabited. The Sunday souk, held just outside the ochre walls, is one of the liveliest in the region. Southeast of the town, a towering natural bridge at **Imi-n-Ifri** carries the road across a boulder-strewn stream. It is a place of gothic fascination, with the cries of crows echoing around the peaks. These are said to be the embodiments of evil spirits who tormented the women of Demnate, only to be transformed by the spirit of the Imi-n-Ifri spring.

Due west of Demnate is the small village of **Tazzerte**, marked by four crumbling kasbahs. A guide will appear to show you round. About 7km further on is the crossroads of **Sidi-Rahhal**, where local saint Sidi Rahhal is buried. The marabout is the focus of a *moussem* in August – his followers are said to have the power of flight, usually preferring carpets as transport.

Demnate: 100km east of Marrakech.
Tazzerte: 47km west of Demnate on Route 6707.

OUKAÏMEDEN

Oukaïmeden means 'the meeting place of the four winds', a name suggesting how cold it can get at an altitude of 2,650m. The road from the Ourika valley zig-zags skywards with views back down the valley and eventually as far as Marrakech. Oukaïmeden is a ski resort, but in summer this is good walking country. Here, too, is a collection of prehistoric rock carvings: a map is available at the Club Alpin chalet (or hire a local guide). The drawings include lightning bolts, hunters, knives and a small elephant. There is a minimal entrance fee to the resort.

72km south of Marrakech.

A room with a view in the white kasbah of Telouet

TIZI-N-TEST

The road rises to the Tizi-n-Test col from Asni to the upper Nfis valley and the ruined Mosque of Tin-Mal. From here it descends 1,600m in 30km – not for the faint-hearted.

Ijoukak

At the head of the high valley of the Nfis, Ijoukak is the gateway to some of Morocco's most beautiful uplands. About 2km south is the ruined kasbah of Talaat n Yacoub, headquarters of the Gondaffi clan. The rival Glaoui clan attacked the kasbah in 1906 when the powerful Gondaffi Caid Si Taieb was absent, and reduced it to its present dilapidated state. Caid Si Taieb returned to find his valley in ruins.
94km south of Marrakech.

Ouirgane

Ouirgane is a convenient lunchtime stopover, comprising two good hotels, one of which arranges horse riding into the hills (see page 162).
60km south of Marrakech.

Tin-Mal

When a Berber theologian, Ibn Toumert, returned to Tin-Mal from Mecca in 1124, he gathered the tribes of the Atlas around him, preaching a message of austerity and piety. His followers formed the Almohad, or Unitarian sect. They amassed to attack the heathen Almoravids, and after Ibn Toumert's death succeeded in capturing Marrakech and Fès. To venerate their founder, they built the mosque at Tin-Mal in 1154. It served as a shrine, but also as a fortress, and was eventually besieged in 1276 by the Merenids, who destroyed the Almohad town but left the mosque, fearful of Ibn Toumert's spirit.

Today it is one of only two mosques in Morocco open to non-Muslims, holding regular Friday services. Its setting is exceptional, above the Nfis river in front of a backdrop of colossal mountains. The roofless and crumbling mosque remains a spiritual place, all the more mystical for its decrepitude.
8km southwest of Ijoukak. Open: sunrise to sunset.

THE GLAOUI

'Lords of the High Atlas', the Glaoui clan rose to power in the late 19th century. They controlled the Tizi-n-Tichka pass, through which Sultan Moulay Hassan returned to Marrakech in 1893. Needing food and water for his depleted army, the Sultan asked brothers Madani and T'hami el Glaoui for assistance, which was lavishly given. In return the Sultan made Madani governor of southern Morocco. In 1907 T'hami became Pasha of Marrakech, ruling from a luxurious palace (see page 92). As a favoured ally of the colonial French powers, he was known as the unofficial 'King of Morocco' for over a decade. In 1953 he attended Queen Elizabeth II's coronation as a guest of Winston Churchill. Ever a shrewd politician, T'hami subsequently realised the French cause was lost and in 1955 he pleaded for the return of Sultan Mohammed V from exile. His rule came to an abrupt end and he died shortly after Moroccan Independence in 1956.

TIZI-N-TICHKA

This breathtaking pass rises to 2,260m, a serpentine road climbing into the clouds. It is a four-hour drive from Marrakech to Ouarzazate – a distance of 204km.

Telouet

The white kasbah of Telouet is a crumbling ruin behind the existing village. In fact it was built by T'hami el Glaoui as recently as 1934 but seems to have been left to disintegrate, symbolising the powerful Glaoui clan's betrayal of Moroccan nationalism, their alliance with the French regime (see box). Guided tours must be taken through the great halls and gaudy reception rooms. Ask to see the harem, kitchens and cinema – the Caid's brother-in-law was actor Edward G Robinson and Hollywood epics were often shown here. On the day of the Caid's death in 1956, over a thousand slaves are said to have fled the kasbah. *21km east of the main P31, 131km southeast of Marrakech.*

The Tizi n'Tichka Pass cuts through some of Morocco's most spectacular scenery

BERBER VILLAGES

Historically, the High Atlas is a region cut off from the outside world. Atlas Berber tribes have never been entirely conquered by occupying forces, and even today the Atlas Berbers pay no tax to the Moroccan government, and receive no state benefits. Yet they are Morocco's indigenous inhabitants, having settled here long before the Arabs from the east. Historians have never successfully determined where they originated – some say in Libya, others the desert further south. Arabic is a foreign language to Berber villagers, who speak their own Tashelhaït dialects.

Berber village life is founded on the basic unit of the extended family. Traditionally, each household or tent was its own republic. When needed, families would band together in confederations to defend the village or reap the harvest.

The Berber architecture of the High Atlas is devoid of the Moorish influences found elsewhere in Morocco: here are simple low stone houses, kasbahs and fortified *agadirs*, or granaries. Although accepting Islam, the Atlas Berbers also embrace more unorthodox religion, and strange geometric designs decorate houses and gateposts, part of a lost magical language. This is the 'other' Morocco, where women are unveiled, working alongside men in the fields.

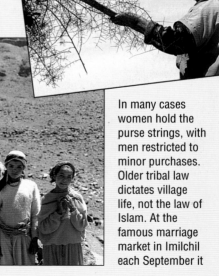

In many cases women hold the purse strings, with men restricted to minor purchases. Older tribal law dictates village life, not the law of Islam. At the famous marriage market in Imilchil each September it

Berber life revolves
around the trinity of the
home, the family and
the fields

is the women who choose
a husband, inspecting the ranks of men
like cattle at market.

But even in this remote world
things are changing. Old black tents are
being replaced with shiny, tin-
roofed houses; school houses are
being built in even the remotest
areas, and you are more likely to
see children with bright school
bags than herds of goats. The
young are leaving the countryside,
seeking a better life in the city.
Depopulation of mountain villages is
leading to the disappearance of
ancient customs and knowledge. One
hope is that the advent of tourism in the
High Atlas will help preserve the Berber
culture – but at what price?

Marrakech Old Town

This walk takes you on a tour through the heart of Imperial Marrakech, ending at one of the world's most luxurious hotels. For the route see the Marrakech town map on page 89. *Allow 4 hours.*

In summer set out early. Begin at Bab Aguenaou, accessible by taxi or a short walk from the Jemaa el Fna.

1 BAB AGUENAOU

The entrance to the kasbah is unmistakable – a monumental block of a gateway, adorned with semi-circular 'sun ray' decorations dating from the reign of Almohad Sultan Yacoub el Mansour.

Pass through the gateway to the square and the walls of the Mosquée d'el Mansour.

2 MOSQUÉE D'EL MANSOUR

This mosque was a contemporary of the Koutoubia, finished in 1190. Now restored by King Hassan to its original Almohad glory, the minaret seems almost modern and excessively gaudy. In fact the bright *Zellij* tiles would also have covered both the Koutoubia and the Tour Hassan in Rabat in their heyday.
Head right along the mosque walls for 20m, past boutiques to the narrow passage leading to the Saadien tombs.

3 SAADIEN TOMBS

Set in fragrant gardens of wild mint, thyme, lemon trees and roses, this small necropolis is a haven of intimacy. First on the left is a richly decorated prayer hall, containing several small tombs. The central masterpiece of the garden is the mausoleum of Ahmed el Mansour, builder of the Palais El Badi. Surrounded by 12 columns and crowned by a fantastically carved dome, it is a fitting resting place for el Debhi, 'the Golden One'. His tomb lies in the middle, flanked by his son and grandson. The other domed koubba houses el Mansour's mother and the mad Sultan Moulay Yazid who died in 1792.
Walk back to Bab Aguenaou on your left, then north 200m to a small roundabout. Here turn right and walk 400m to place des Ferblantiers, where you pass through an arch and head for the entrance of the El Badi.

4 PALAIS EL BADI

Constructed by Saadian Sultan Ahmed el Mansour with money from gold plundered in Timbuktu, this was once one of the finest palaces in the world.

Reflections of past glory in the pool of the El Badi palace

While travelling Italy, French philosopher Montaigne was surprised to see craftsmen carving great pillars of marble for 'the king of Fès and Barbary' (see page 92).
Pass back via place des Ferblantiers, through the arch on the left and north 400m along rue Riad Zitoun el Kedim to Jemaa el Fna.

5 JEMAA EL FNA

Jemaa el Fna is the meeting place for the city's best entertainers, merchants and pickpockets (see page 90). For an enthralling view of the pandemonium, climb to the terrace of Café de la Place or Café Glacier and enjoy the spectacle with a glass of mint tea.
Walk 250m southwest from the Jemaa to place Youssef Ben Tachfine.

6 KOUTOUBIA

The earliest of Almohad minarets, the Koutoubia is the symbol of Marrakech and a model for subsequent building (see page 91). The minaret of the Hassan II mosque in Casablanca is a direct descendant.
Follow avenue Houmann el Fetouaki 300m west to the Mamounia hotel, on the left.

7 HOTEL MAMOUNIA

A former palace, the Mamounia was converted into a hotel in the 1920s. This was Winston Churchill's favourite hotel and his personal suite remains in its original style, complete with paintings, books and hat. Today the Mamounia continues to welcome politicians, film stars and lesser mortals to its recently redecorated luxury. A drink in the bar or garden is just about affordable (see page 94).
Take a taxi back to your hotel.

Marrakech to Ourika

A popular excursion to the villages of the High
Atlas and the fertile valley of the Ourika river.
*The 135km round-trip can last a whole day taken
at a leisurely pace. Those pushed for time can
make it to Setti-Fatma and back in half a day. In spring
beware of flooding.*

From Marrakech take the S513, signposted Ouriki, Setti Fatma.

1 DAR-CAÏD-OURIKI

The road south from Marrakech is flat and uninteresting until
Dar-Caid-Ouriki, 33km down the road.
This hamlet marks the beginning of the
valley and hosts a Monday souk.
Traditionally it has been the trading post
for Atlas donkeys, which are bought and
sold at auction; today pottery and hunks
of coloured rock are more in evidence on
the market stalls.

*The road continues 10km to the turn-off to
Oukaïmeden.*

2 THE OURIKA VALLEY

This narrow valley is cut by Oued
Ourika, a river originating 3,600m up in
the High Atlas. It is a place of abundant
greenery, farmed terraces and fruit trees,
populated by villages of ochre stone
houses. When the aridity of summer
turns Marrakech into an unbearable heat
bowl, the Ourika Valley is cool, brushed
by mountain breezes. In the past no
ruler of Marrakech could afford to
ignore the wishes of the inhabitants of
the Ourika: they controlled the water
supply to the city. Today Marrakechis
flock to its shady orchards and gentle
streams. Along the way look out for the
carefully constructed irrigation channels,

The fertile valley of the Ourika, watered by High Atlas snows

or seguias, feeding vegetable gardens. In spring these channels overflow, and stories abound of wily Berbers selling vast tracts of land to foreign real-estate companies, only for the land to be ravaged by floods the next spring and bought back at half the price. In March and April the valley floor is awash with colour as the cherry, plum, apple and almond trees blossom.

3 ARHBALOU

The end of the line for most locals, Arhbalou offers a scattering of shops and a hotel-restaurant. There is also a small 'museum' of local crafts, which doubles as a gift shop. The drive can be extended to take in the ski resort of Oukaïmeden (see page 99), by turning a further 29km up hair-pin bends on Route 6035.
Continue along the S513 from Arhbalou a further 24km south to the end of the valley and Setti-Fatma.

4 SETTI-FATMA

From Arhbalou Route S513 follows the river between rocky hillsides coated with Holm oaks. A kilometre before Setti-

Fatma the road peters out and a path crossed by mountain streams leads up to the village. Above the houses are seven waterfalls, which if rains have been plentiful plunge into deep pools. Barbary monkeys are said to live in the surrounding hills, feeding off the walnut trees that shade the waterfalls.

Above the river a small path leads up to the green-roofed tomb of Lalla Setti-Fatma, the village saint. This is the site of one of the biggest *moussem* in the High Atlas, which usually takes place in mid-August.
Eat lunch in Setti-Fatma or head back north to Marrakech.

Mount Toubkal

Set in the wild and beautiful Toubkal National Park, this region of the High Atlas is easily accessible from Marrakech, and is a must for those who enjoy hiking and the exhilaration of mountain scenery. An ascent of the third highest mountain in Africa, the highest in North Africa, is feasible for anyone of average fitness. It is best climbed between May and October. *Set out from Marrakech early to arrive mid-morning at Imlil. The climb to Neltner refuge takes about five hours. You then sleep the night in the refuge, waking at dawn for the three-hour ascent to the 4,167m peak of Toubkal. Descend to the shelter where you could spend another night, or head back directly to Imlil.*

Remember to pack warm clothing, even in summer, as nights and early mornings are cold. It is advisable to hire a guide for the walk and perhaps mules to carry baggage. Both guides and mules are available at Imlil. You will need strong shoes or boots, sunglasses and a hat, and sleeping bags (rented at Imlil). Take your time over the ascent as altitude sickness is not uncommon.

1 IMLIL

Surrounding Imlil the mountains exude an ancient silence, a world away from the vivacity of Marrakech. This tiny hamlet, already at 1700m, centres on a wide square where you can hire guides, buy provisions and swap hiking stories with walkers just returned from Toubkal. It is best to set out before lunch.

The track leads through chestnut woods to the right of the village and up to a dirt road leading past the Berber village of Aremd, dark slate houses clinging to the hillside. Cross the wide plain of the Mizane and ascend the east slopes where the path leads high above the river.

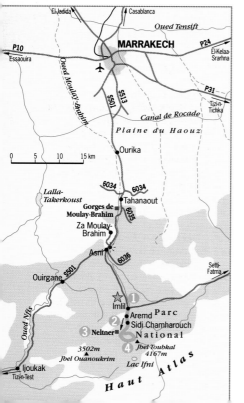

From Imlil the path climbs to the summit of Toubkal, Africa's third highest mountain

2 SIDI CHAMHAROUCH

The white domed marabout of Sidi Chamharouch is 1½ hours (3km) from Aremd. This small settlement is a good place to rest, buy provisions and pat yourself on the back. Moroccan pilgrims make the journey here by donkey to worship at the marabout. The strange bare tree before the village is said to be magical and is sometimes decorated with rags.

It takes roughly three hours (4km) from Sidi Chamharouch to the Neltner refuge on a serpentine path which ascends to a higher valley. At the end of the valley is the refuge.

3 NELTNER REFUGE

At 3,207m, this small refuge marks the spring snow line. Very busy in summer, it can be cramped, but the atmosphere is always welcoming and tall tales of epic treks abound. The old *gardien* will usually cook you *tajine*, or pasta. Bottled water and biscuits are also available.

The final 1,000m to the summit begin behind the refuge. The first climb is the hardest: a steep ascent over large boulders which then turn to scree further up. There are two paths to the top – the easier of these swings right before following the crest of the range to Mount Toubkal.

4 MOUNT TOUBKAL

The view from the 4,167m summit is breathtaking, literally so if the wind is blowing. The best time to experience being the highest person in North Africa is early morning when the light is clear and you can see as far as the desert to the south and Marrakech to the north.

Descend the same route to Neltner, and from there to Imlil. Going down is easier.

Essaouira to Agadir

From the romantic fishing port of Essaouira to the international resort of Agadir, this drive takes you along a stretch of Morocco's wildest and most beautiful coastline. *Allow 3 hours for the 173km one-way drive.*

From Essaouira the P8 leads out of town along the sea front to join the main P8 south to Agadir; 12km south the 6604 turns right to Sidi Kaouki and Cap Sim.

1 CAP SIM

Sidi Kaouki and the sand dunes of Cap Sim are home to a large domed *marabout* and one of the world's best wind-surfing beaches. The spirit of Sidi Kaouki is said to cure infertility, but most of the camper vans are here for the surf. Camels can be hired for treks into the dunes.

The province of Haha is the western limb of the Atlas mountains and a stronghold of the Tachelhaït Berber language and culture. The hills descend almost to the sea, where high cliffs plunge down to beach coves. The Atlas foothills are covered with argan, a strange thorny tree indigenous to Morocco which produces an orange fruit much sought after by local goats, who climb up the trees to feed. Local Berbers grind the argan nut to make a sweet oil – these nuts are 'harvested' from the dung of goats.

The Tachelhaït Berbers have long been reputed for their independent spirit. Even today, if you turn off the main road you will come across villages where neither Arabic nor French is spoken.

Return along the 6604 to rejoin the P8 south.

2 SMIMOU AND JBEL AMSITTEN

Smimou, 40km south of Cap Sim, offers a petrol station and several cafés. About 8km further south, the narrow Route 6633 heads left up into the hills, past thuya and argan forests to 905m Jbel Amsitten, and a watchtower offering a memorable view across the Haha and up to the peaks of the High Atlas.

Continue along the P8 to Tamanar; 16km beyond is a small road to the sea and Pointe Imessouane.

3 POINTE IMESSOUANE

This small Berber fishing village is relaxed and friendly and is now a favourite base for windsurfers and surfers. A small auberge offers beds and a wonderful sea view. It is usually possible to pay a fisherman to take you on a tour of the rocky coast – pack a picnic, cast a fishing line and snooze the day away

30km south the P8 rejoins the coast at Tamri and its extensive banana plantation

4 TARHAZOUT

The road climbs over Cap Rhir, the last spur of the High Atlas before the fertile plain of the Sous. The beach at Amesnaz is safe for swimming, as is that at Tarhazout, much loved by modern-day hippies in the winter and Moroccan families in the summer. Beyond, the hamlet of Tamraht is nicknamed 'Banana Village' for its stalls of the local speciality, small pink bananas.

From the centre of Tamrakht Route 7002 leads up into the hills and the waterfalls at Imouzzer-Ida-Outanan.

Persistent goats search for Argan nuts along the road to Agadir

5 IMOUZZER-IDA-OUTANAN

Once past the banana plantations of Tamraht, the palm-lined gorge is appropriately named 'Paradise Valley'. Beyond, the road climbs to Imouzzer, a whitewashed village famed for its honey (see **Festivals**, page 156). Below the village is a series of waterfalls, reduced by recent drought and irrigation to the merest of trickles. The walk is enticing enough though, leading to a large pool where divers attempt to earn coins by pirouetting into its depths.

From Imouzzer-Ida-Outanan it is 61km to Agadir, back via the P8.

The South

Vast green palm oases, red sand, blue men and camel trains – the south of Morocco goes a long way to realising most dreams of Arabian and African exoticism. Like all of Morocco it is a place of abundant variety, from the modern tourist metropolis of Agadir, via the red pisé Ksour of the Vallée du Dra (Dra Valley) to the great sand dunes of Erg Chebbi.

While most visitors are based in Agadir, with its unrivalled infrastructure of hotels, beach clubs and restaurants, the real jewels of the south are found in the smaller towns and villages of the fertile Plaine du Sous (Sous plain), the Anti Atlas and the southern oasis valleys. From these arid outposts came the warriors of the Sahara: the Almoravids in the 11th century and the Saadians, who swept north to conquer Marrakech and Fès in the 16th century.

A fiercely proud people, the Berbers of southern Morocco have since conquered much of the country through their economic prowess – the merchants and shopkeepers of the Sous are renowned for their business sense. Most Moroccan businessmen abroad originated in this region. The indigenous Chleuh Berber are distinct from other Moroccans: their features are well-defined, seeming almost oriental. Famous for their energy and dexterity, the Chleuh are the best acrobats and dancers in the country. The south is, above all, a relaxed place, a land closer to the joie de vivre of Africa than the conservatism of Europe and the Middle East.

Do not miss the ancient Saadien capital of Taroudannt, or the striking villages of the Ameln valley near Tafraout, with their almond orchards and bizarre rock formations. Travel south down the ancient caravan routes of the Dra and Ziz valleys. If you have time, head east to the greatest oasis in Morocco, the desert border town of Figuig – you will not be disappointed.

AGADIR

Once a peaceful trading post, exporting sugar and cotton from the Sous valley, Agadir is now famous as Morocco's number one tourist resort. Yet few holidaymakers realise that Agadir is the scene of one of Morocco's greatest tragedies. In just 15 seconds at midnight on 29 February 1960, 15,000 people were killed and the town wiped out by a massive earthquake. As rescue workers tried to dig out bodies, cholera

Rocky cliffs and lengthy sands characterise the coast north of Agadir

Rare sea birds holiday on the Oued Souss estuary outside Agadir

spread and it was decided to bury the city and its dead, and to begin again. In the words of Mohammed V, New Agadir is a testament to the 'faith and determination' of its inhabitants and the Moroccan people.

There are few sights. You come here to do one thing: lie on the beach. Fifty per cent of all Morocco's tourist revenue is said to come from Agadir alone. The town is ultra-modern, with relatively tasteful hotels and apartment blocks lining the beach (they are all reassuringly earthquake-proof). The kasbah, north of the port, is all that remains of the old town. From here there is a good view around the bay, north to the industrial quarter and south to the newly constructed royal palace.

Heading along rue de la Corniche, you pass a hillock on the right, now planted with trees. This is the burial mound from 1960, a strangely impersonal memorial to the dead.

Further on is the port and a series of tables and stalls where you can buy fish fresh from the trawlers, have it fried and eat it on the quayside. Agadir is the biggest sardine port in the world, but there are many other fishy varieties, from squid to shark.

In the town itself the Municipal Museum on avenue Mohammed V has a passable display of southern Moroccan arts and crafts.

The sandy beach is the main focus of life in Agadir. Here you can sail, water-ski, scuba-dive, fish, windsurf and ride camels to your hearts content. Or simply lie in the sun for an average of 300 days each year.

273km southwest of Marrakech, 511km south of Casablanca.
Tourist Office: place Heritier Sidi Mohammed (tel: 82 28 94).
Musée Municipal, avenue Mohammed V. Open: 9.30am–1pm and 2.30pm–6pm. Admission charge.

An orange specialist at the Guelmime market

AGADIR ENVIRONS

Guelmime

A dusty desert gateway, Guelmime was the last stop on a Saharan caravan route that led from Mali and Ghana to the Atlantic. By the 8th century it was site of a large market, where West African gold was exchanged for Saharan salt. As late as 1920, slaves were still brought here from villages in Mali and Upper Volta to be shipped to Europe.

Today Guelmime is an uninteresting administration post, enlivened by a 'traditional' camel market each Saturday. In the past this must have been a dramatic sight, with long trains of camels arriving at dawn, serenaded by their drivers. Today, bus loads of tourists arrive after breakfast – the camels are sold not for transport but for meat. Orchestrating the show are 'blue men' – Berber desert nomads who dress in blue robes which leave a trace of blue dye on their skins (see pages 116–17). Most blue men are in fact locals, dressing up for the occasion. The camel market does not take place in summer.
199km south of Agadir.

Sidi-Ifni

When the Spanish departed this enclave, as recently as 1969, they left a ghost town of art deco buildings, including an Andalusian garden, a Catholic church and a consulate, which still hint at past decadence and colonial luxury. The port is now thriving once more, and the town is a relaxed stopover point, with gentle sea mists adding to the ghostly ambience.
165km south of Agadir. Souk: Sunday.

Tafraout

A string of *pisé* villages nestles in a valley of oases beneath curious twisted rock formations (see page 128). East of Tafraout is a barren land punctuated by oases. Tata is the main base in this exceptionally beautiful region, while 62km south, at Akka, lurk some of the most impressive prehistoric rock carvings in North Africa (you will need a local guide to find them).

Tafraout: 144km southeast of Agadir, souk: Wednesday. Tata: 242km southeast of Taroudannt, souk: Thursday and Sunday.

Taliouine and Tazenakht

Two stopovers on the main route between Agadir and Ouarzazate, these villages are often overlooked by visitors. Taliouine lies above a deep valley of scattered villages and almond orchards. In the valley is the ruined Glaoui kasbah, a palace guarded by four square towers. From Taliouine a five-day hike leads to 3,304m Jbel Siroua, a volcanic cone dominating the Anti-Atlas range.

Further east, Tazenakht is a centre for carpets woven by the Ouzguita tribe. A small co-operative opens its doors to the curious, and you can see the bold geometric designs being woven.

Taliouine: 200km east of Agadir. Tazenakht: 285km east of Agadir.

Taroudannt

Meaning 'town of the pinnacles', Taroudannt is famous for its red crenallated walls. It is a prosperous market town that was once headquarters of the Saadian dynasty (see page 126).

80km east of Agadir.

Tiznit

Tiznit is a 'new town', founded in the 1880s when Sultan Moulay Hassan surrounded disparate kasbahs within 5km of pink walls. In 1912 a local chief, El Hiba, proclaimed himself Sultan and set forth with an army to face the French, who had just taken Fès. 'The Blue Sultan', named for his exotic desert robes, was defeated after Marrakech and returned to exile and death near Tafraout.

The town is famous for its jewellery – its *mechouar* was home to Jewish artisans, who began a tradition of silver work that continues today. North of the souks is the Grand Mosque and the Source Lalla Tiznit, shrine to a local ex-prostitute who was martyred for Islam. A spring appeared where she fell and flows to this day.

There is an impressive beach west of Tiznit at **Aglou**.

91km south of Agadir. Souk: Thursday.

Farmers riding into Taroudannt for the market

BLUE MEN

Ashimmering apparition on the distant horizon, a handsome warrior in flowing blue robes astride a magnificent camel: this is the fabled vision of a 'Blue Man', the fearsome nomad of the Sahara. Today it is little more than a dream – nearly all blue men you meet are impostors, dressing up for the tourists.

Authentic blue men come from the southern fringes of Morocco. They belong to the Rguibat Berbers, a nomadic tribe which used to rely on goat and sheep farming, and occasional raids on the caravans that crossed the Sahara. They are related to the Tuareg, who live in western Algeria and Mauritania, with whom they often fought (there are no Tuareg in Morocco, despite elaborate claims). The Rguibat wear bright blue robes, the men sporting a blue veil and scarf wrapped tightly around the head to keep out sand. Originally this blue was a dark indigo, imported, so myth states, by a Scottish merchant to Agadir in the 16th century. The indigo washed onto the skin, turning the men blue. It was prized as a symbol of wealth – indigo was expensive. Today the blue headscarves are all synthetic. In the past the men would also paint their eyelids green before they rode into battle to frighten their foe. The women are famed for the *guedra*, an erotic dance performed squatting amid a circle of men (see page 155).

Renowned for their skill with horse and camel, the blue men made a good living offering 'protection' to camel trains between the Atlantic and Mauritania. Camels were the lifeblood of the Sahara: in 1946 there were 100,000 in southern Morocco.

In the last century an American sailor was part of a caravan of 4,000 camels and 1,000 men heading to Timbuktu. On the way they were attacked by a band of blue men – he recorded that only 21 men and 12 camels eventually reached their destination.

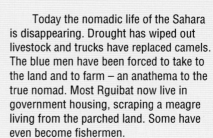

The majestic blue men of the Sahara, now little more than a tourist gimmick

Today the nomadic life of the Sahara is disappearing. Drought has wiped out livestock and trucks have replaced camels. The blue men have been forced to take to the land and to farm – an anathema to the true nomad. Most Rguibat now live in government housing, scraping a meagre living from the parched land. Some have even become fishermen.

The kasbah of Ait Benhaddou, star of many Hollywood movies

AÏT BENHADDOU

Of all the southern kasbahs, palm-fringed
Aït Benhaddou is the most impressive,
backed by a hilltop *agadir*. If you sense
you have seen it before, do not be
surprised. It has starred in six films and
numerous fashion articles. The main
gateway, which seems so well preserved,
was actually restored by a film company.
Despite such exposure the village
remains relaxed. In the past this was a
major halt on the gold route between
Marrakech and the Sahara. In times of
siege the inhabitants would withdraw to
the fortified *agadir* (the pisé walls offered
little protection – they could be
destroyed simply by diverting the stream
to run beneath them). In peace time the
valley was farmed as it is today, although
tourists have replaced gold as the
village's main source of income.
Children await visitors crossing the
valley, offering to show off their houses.
32km north of Ouarzazate.

EL-KELAA-M'GOUNA

At the meeting place of the M'Gouna
and Dades valleys, El-Kelaa-M'Gouna is
famous for its roses. Here, at an altitude
of 2,000m, the fields are divided by
hedgerows of rose bushes which in May
and early June burst forth into a
proliferation of colour. The roses are
harvested and processed at the Cappet
Floral factory to make rose water, a liquid
much prized in the Arab world for
ablutions before meals. The dried rose
petals can be seen in many of the
country's spice souks . The rose harvest is
accompanied by a large *moussem.*

An excursion up the valley to the small
hamlet of Bou Thrarar leads through the
rose fields, along the side of steep cliffs to
villages rarely visited by tourists.
92km northeast of Ouarzazate.

ER-RACHIDIA

Er-Rachidia is capital of the Tafilalt
region, a valley system on the edge of the
Sahara famed for its vast date palm oases.
Built by the French Foreign Legion in the
early 20th century, it was originally known
as Ksar es Souk but following
independence was renamed after Moulay
Rachid, founder of the present-day
Alaouite dynasty.

Er-Rachidia has always been of strategic importance, where the roads from Algeria, Fès and Marrakech meet, and even today there is a large military presence in the town. This is also an area of great agricultural development: following floods in 1960, which destroyed villages and crops, dams were built and the oases of Er-Rachidia are now highly profitable. The town is a good base for transport south to the Gorges du Ziz (Ziz gorge). In October the region comes alive for the annual date *moussem*.

358km south of Fès, 510km east of Marrakech. Souk: Sunday.

FIGUIG

Figuig lies in an amphitheatre of dark mountains, where 200,000 palm trees fill the valley. Historically it has been a stopover on the pilgrimage route to Mecca, a pious but relaxed town. The border and Algeria lie just 3km to the south. Figuig has been fought over by Algeria and Morocco for centuries, the last time in 1975 when border units skirmished in the streets. Today all is quiet.

It can get very hot here and any sightseeing should be done early. Seven *ksour* command the oasis, signposted off the main road. These fortified settlements have fought more among themselves than with outsiders, for control of precious water rights. **El Maiz** is the most accessible and prettiest, while **El Hammam** encloses a hot spring. **El-Oudarhir**, at the oasis entrance, also has mineral springs. Furthest from the main centre, **Zenaga** is the richest and most elegant of the *ksour*.

376km south of Oujda, 385km east of Er-Rachidia. Souk: Wednesday and Saturday.

Right: the oasis of Tafilalt
Below: the ornamental gateway to Er Rachidia

Countless kasbahs line the valley of the Dadès, in the foothills of the High Atlas mountains

as most people get, 25km from Boumalne: it is a good base for hiking. A track leads right round to the Todra gorge, accessible only by four-wheel drive. *116km northeast of Ouarzazate.*

GORGES DU TODRA

A sharp faultline in the plateau separating the High Atlas from the Anti Atlas, the Todra gorge is not as extensive as the neighbouring Dadès, but for a short distance it is more spectacular. Take route 6902 north through the Tinerhir palm oasis (see page 122) and into the narrow canyon, where 300m-high cliffs descend to the river bed. The road continues to a small group of hotels cowering under a vast lip of rock. From here the track leads onwards through a great scar cut by the rock – in spring, when the river is full, this section lives up to its name of 'the jaws of hell'. Here rock climbers dangle from the cliffs, birdwatchers count rare species and rafters hurtle by. If possible, spend a night in one of the hotels – dusk and dawn are the most poignant moments in the gorges. *181km northeast of Ouarzazate.*

IMILCHIL

North of the Dadès and Todra gorges, the mountain tracks become more precarious and should only be attempted in Landrovers. From Msemrir or Aït Hani it is roughly 100km north to the plateau of Imilchil. Imilchil is famous for its September marriage market, when the semi-nomadic Aït Haddidou tribe descends from the uplands for a harvest festival with a difference. Unmarried or divorced women, recognisable from their pointed bonnets, choose a partner from

GORGES DU DADÈS

The 'Sabre Cut' is aptly named: a steep incision into the foothills of the Atlas forms the gorge, accessible by car along tarmac and then reasonable gravel. It is a spectacular drive, from the moment you turn off at Boumalne. The gorge is wide at first, as you pass a ruined Glaoui kasbah. Palm trees do not grow at this altitude, but almonds and poplars line the valley. As the gorge steepens and the road becomes more serpentine the rocks are transformed into strange shapes, towering spears and proud mushrooms. At **Aït Arbi** the cluster of kasbahs lurks beneath a bulbous rock outcrop, poetically named 'the brain of the Atlas'. Further on are the 'hills of the human bodies', with foot-like protrusions jutting from the cliffside. **Aït Oudinar** is as far

A lonely outpost at the foot of the Todra gorge

ranks of disgruntled men. The village itself is pretty, and offers beautiful walks to the Plateau des Lacs. Twin lakes, said to have been formed by the tears of two unrequited lovers from rival tribes, are the reason for the marriage market – **Lac Tislit** (Lake of the Bride) and **Lac Isli** (Lake of the Groom). An alternative route leads from Midelt (see page 74). *180km west of Midelt 92km north of Tinerhir.*

Storks coming home to roost in Ouarzazate

OUARZAZATE

Advertised as the gateway to the Sahara, Ouarzazate is a friendly yet uninspiring town. The main sight is the Glaoui Taourirt kasbah, to the southeast of the centre, a fortress of cinematic proportions. The courtyard contains a German cannon used to spread the influence of the Glaoui throughout the south. Inside, the ghostly rooms still contain *Zellij* decorations and painted plasterwork, but as the wind blows from the Sahara the rooms seem doomed to disappear under the sands of time (open: 8.30am–noon, 2pm–6.30pm; admission charge). Opposite is a well-stocked Ensemble Artisinal, specialising in local Berber carpets.

The climate and dramatic landscapes of the south have attracted the attentions of Hollywood. Ouarzazate now boasts its own Atlas film studios, 6km north of the centre, where you can see a fighter plane used by Michael Douglas and an army of jeeps that chased James Bond. The studio hotel is open when crews are not filming here. *204km southeast of Marrakech. Souk: Sunday.*

SKOURA

The oasis of Skoura appears suddenly from the barren landscape, marking the entrance to the Dadès Valley, 'the valley of a thousand kasbahs.' The first kasbah – the kasbah of Amerhidl – is before Skoura village, 500m to the left of the road. From Skoura, a maze of paths criss-crosses the oasis, lined with irrigation canals leading to ochre kasbahs.

42km northeast of Ouarzazate. Souk: Monday, Thursday.

TINERHIR

A former French Foreign Legion garrison, Tinerhir hosts a large oasis and a Glaoui kasbah. It is a good base for exploring the Todra Gorge, or a pleasant stopover between Ouarzazate and Er-Rachidia.

169km east of Ouarzazate. Souk: Tuesday.

A Tinerhir shopkeeper and the bargain of the month

FANCY A DATE?

The date palm is a vital mainstay of the southern oases. Without it there would be no settlements south of the Atlas: dates are the region's most profitable crop. The palm branches provide shade for all other crops, while the tree's roots hold the soil together in fierce desert winds. Palm wood is used to build pisé houses, branches carpet most floors and wood scraps are used as kindling for fires. There are over four million date palms in the southern oases, producing 100,000 tonnes of dates a year. The best eating dates are found at Zagora (others are used for animal feed). Harvest takes place in late October, when roads are lined with children selling boxes of the succulent fruit. The date palm is sacred in Islam: the Koran describes Jesus' birth among palm trees. This symbol of fertility is often found tattooed on women's hands. Because of its sanctity, the palm is protected: in the past it was forbidden to sell a living tree, and harvesting was strictly regulated by holy elders. Yet times have changed. Recent drought and the ravages caused by Bayoud Palm sickness, a fungus which spreads among roots, has meant that tourism is rapidly overtaking dates as the main industry of the south.

VALLÉE DU DRA

The Dra valley is a string of oases following one of the Sahara's great river valleys. Around 80,000 people live on this thin strip of land, farming the rich palm groves. Tourism is apparent but always on the fringes (see page 130).

M'hamid

You no longer need an official permit to drive to the end of the road at the edge of the Sahara. A dusty town with little to see, M'hamid cherishes its visitors: tours are offered to the 'dunes' to the west.
91km south of Zagora, 255km southeast of Ouarzazate. Souk: Monday.

Tamgrout

Tamgrout possesses one of the few Islamic libraries open to non-Muslims, in a modern building to the right of the main street from the P31. The library contains volumes of the Koran that are over 700 years old written on gazelle hide. Near by, a courtyard of the restored *zaouia* is accessible, where the infirm still gather seeking salvation from the local saint. Down the road is an interesting pottery co-operative (see page 147).
13km south of Zagora. Souk: Saturday.

Tinfou

The one tame sand dune in the Dra, Tinfou seems to have been dropped there by mistake. The dune rises 20m, surrounded by a flat plain, and is best seen at dawn or dusk. The adherent 'blue men' are far from authentic.
7km south of Tamgrout.

Zagora

A dusty oasis town, Zagora has little to offer other than a good base for exploring the surrounding, and much more interesting countryside (see page 131).
164km southeast of Ouarzazate. Souk: Wednesday, Sunday.

The banks of the Dra River where crocodiles once roamed

ZIZ, GORGES DU

The second of the great southern oasis valleys, the Ziz is a mere 80km from the Algerian border. From here came the Alaouite dynasty, still in power today, and during French occupation the Foreign legion used the area as its main stronghold. Today the great oasis of Tafilalt and the sand dunes of Erg Chebbi make it one of the most memorable regions in Morocco.

Erfoud

As with many settlements in the Ziz, Erfoud was founded by the French Foreign Legion in 1917 as a base from which to control the Tafilalt oasis. It has little to offer other than being a good

Choosing the right vegetable at the Erfoud market

starting point for visiting the sand dunes further south. Borj Est, a fort still occupied by the Moroccan army, provides a panoramic view south to the sand, and north across a sea of palms to the Atlas (from behind the main square, cross Bab el Oued and a track leads 2km up to the fort).

79km south of Er-Rachidia, 290km northeast of Ouarzazate. Souk: Saturday.

Merzouga – Erg Chebbi

Erg Chebbi is what draws most people to the Ziz. From Erfoud route 3461 leads past Borj Est and continues a further 55km to the sand dunes. It is advisable to set out before dawn, to see the red dunes catch fire at sunrise. The road becomes desert track after 17km and you must follow a series of telegraph poles (if in doubt, hire a guide in Erfoud to accompany you. Beware of sand storms and heavy rain which tends to incapacitate non four-wheel drive cars). An alternative base to Erfoud is the huddle of *auberges* at the foot of the dunes, which provide basic food and accommodation.

The dunes themselves start 33km south of Erfoud, a spectacular sight at any time, rising to 150m. Skirting the dunes, you arrive at **Merzouga**, with a handful of hotels. West of the hamlet is **Dayet Sriji**, a seasonal lake which attracts pink flamingos in winter months – an unforgettable sight.

Merzouga: 57km south of Erfoud. Souk: Saturday.

Meski

The French Foreign Legion, tired of dying of bilharzia and being shot at, decided to build a walled swimming pool where they could enjoy a dip in relative security. The source bleue de Meski is a

The blue source of the Meski River

natural spring and a favourite stopover point on the road south to Erfoud. The cement basin is still clean, the water flowing freely, but the oasis solitude enjoyed by the legionnaires has been transformed into a crowded campsite.
23km south of Er-Rachidia, 56km north of Erfoud. Admission charge to site.

Rissani

At the heart of the Tafilalt oasis, Rissani is a windswept, forgotten settlement among bowing palm trees. Its 17th-century kasbah is a maze of streets populated by shrouded figures, many of whom claim to belong to the Alaouite dynasty of King Hassan II. Just west of the village are the ruins of **Sijilmassa**, now little more than submerged walls. For a thousand years this was the principal trading post for caravans from the Niger river which deposited great piles of gold in return for salt and sugar. Today nothing is left.

The mausoleum of the first Alaouite ruler, Moulay Ali Cherif, lies 2km south of Rissani, rebuilt in 1955 after floods. It is surprisingly subdued, and not open to non-Muslims. More impressive is the

Flag day at the grand gateway entrance to Rissani

Kasbah Oulad Abdelhalim, just beyond the mausoleum, which was built in 1900 as a palace for the Sultan's brother.

Rissani only comes to life on market days. Then, donkeys mass the small square and the kasbah is resurrected from the dead. On other days, three boutiques sell Berber carpets and jewellery.
22km south of Erfoud. Souk: Sunday, Tuesday, Thursday.

Agadir to Taroudannt

This country drive takes you to one of the most impressive architectural sights in the south: the red walls and imposing battlements of Taroudannt, one-time capital of Saadien Morocco. *It is 80km from Agadir to Taroudannt; set out early as possible to avoid midday heat and to return in the evening.*

Take the P32 east of Agadir (signpost Aït-Melloul/Ouarzazate) through the forest of Ademine and the orange and olive groves of the Sous valley. The road crosses Oued Sous, north of Adouar, and after 6km, Taroudannt is on your left.

TAROUDANNT

The first thing you notice about Taroudannt is its walls – majestic ochre battlements against a backdrop of High Atlas mountains. The crenellated edifices are among the best preserved in Morocco, rambling for 7km around the city. The town was occupied in 1056, when the Almoravids conquered the Sous, but remained a provincial market town until the Saadians built their fortified capital in 1554. The walls are made of *pisé* – desert earth baked by the sun and reinforced with straw and wood from palm trees. In places, large fissures are visible, caused by the Agadir earthquake of 1960.

RAMPART TOUR

The best way to see the ramparts is by horse-drawn *calèche* or by bicycle. The tour takes about 30 minutes, and is most enjoyable at dusk when the walls glow in the setting sun. Bicycles are available from opposite the Taroudannt Hotel on

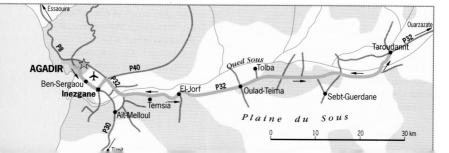

place Assareg and from Hotel Palais Salam, south of the centre, which is also a base for the *calèches*. Settle on a price before ascending your carriage.

PLACE ASSAREG AND PLACE TALMOKLATE

All roads in Taroudannt lead to the two main squares, place Assareg to the north and place Talmoklate to the south, connected by the town's main street. Place Assareg is the hub of action with hotels, restaurants, shops and banks, and a good place to park your car. Some buses use place Talmoklate.

THE SOUKS

To get to the souks, take the road south from the Banque Marocaine in place Assareg (the huddle of streets is small and easily negotiable). Local specialities include silver jewellery from the pre-Sahara and limestone carvings influenced by African folklore. Fur hats are an incongruous addition; they are made from foxes, which stalk the Sous valley.

THE TANNERIES

To the left from the bus station on place Assareg, a street leads north past Hotel Taroudannt to the ramparts. Here, at Bab Khemis, turn left for 100m and the tanneries are on the right. Placed outside the walls, due to the aroma of cattle urine and pigeon droppings used to cure the skins, the tanneries are small and subdued, compared with those of Fès and Marrakech.

HÔTEL PALAIS SALAM

A converted 18th-century palace, the Palais Salam hides away against the battlements at the centre of the kasbah quarter. Now a fashionable watering-hole for media types, its palm tree garden is

Taroudant was a stronghold of resistance against the French

an unforgettable location for a beer or mint tea (see page 173).

LA GAZELLE D'OR

Built for Baron von Pellenc in 1938 as a holiday retreat, La Gazelle d'Or is described by many as the most exclusive hotel in Morocco, located on the route d'Amezgou, 2km south of town. Orange and olive groves adorn the gardens, and non-residents can enjoy a taste of paradise at the bar/terrace, where Morocco's most expensive mint tea is also one of its best (see page 173). *Return to Agadir after sunset, having toured the ramparts.*

Agadir to Tafraout

This round trip from Agadir takes you to the small Berber villages of the Vallée des Ameln (Ameln valley), and the remarkable red rock of Tafraout. The route heads south against the backdrop of the Anti Atlas mountains, past verdant oases and dark, jagged hills, and the scattered settlements of the Ameln Berbers, one of Morocco's most ancient tribes. *The 345km round trip can be accomplished in a day, although a stopover in Tafraout allows more time to explore. Remember to set out early to avoid midday heat in summer. Take plenty of drinking water and check you have a good spare tyre.*

Head south from Agadir to Inezgane and Aït-Melloul, from where you take the S509 southeast to Aït-Baha and Tafraout.

1 AÏT-BAHA

An unassuming village 82km from Agadir, Aït-Baha is a good place to break your journey for refreshment. South of here, the road starts to wind into the mountains beneath spectacular ochre peaks, providing some of the most impressive views in Morocco. **Troulit**, 40km from Aït-Baha, is a dramatic village, dominated by a craggy fortress. This is the domain of the Illalen, a group of 18 tribes who command the mountain plateau. Beyond, the 1,500m **Tizi-n-Taraktine pass** is the gateway to the Ameln valley.

At the pass keep right as the road forks: the left-hand road leads back north to Irhem.

2 TAFRAOUT

As the road descends you will see the first granite outcrops, a lunar landscape of red and purple rock formed by the cooling of lava flows. These weird and wonderful formations reminded writer Paul Bowles of the badlands of South Dakota, 'writ on a grand scale'. Tafraout itself is located by a large oasis, a convenient base to explore the villages of the Ameln valley, and a good place to eat lunch and buy provisions. South of Tafraout are the painted rocks of **Agard Oudad**.

3 AGARD OUDAD

Famous for its pastel houses at the foot of the massive 'Napoleon's hat' rock, Agard Oudad is 3km south of Tafraout on the small route 7075. Head a further 3km southwest (the tarmac becomes dirt track) to a desert landscape much favoured by film directors, and bizarre blue and red rocks painted by Belgian artist Jean Vérame in 1985.

The Ameln valley is north of Tafraout: head back towards Agadir on S509 until Oumesnat. This is the start of the valley – 27 villages extending 40km.

4 OUMESNAT

Perched at the foot of the soaring cliff of Jbel Lekst, Oumesnat is a cluster of houses hugging the mountain, including

The blue and red rocks of Agard Oudad

Granite cliffs dwarf the colourful villages of the Ameln valley

one transformed into a small 'museum'. Most villages in the valley are empty of young men, who have left to seek success in Casablanaca and abroad. They return to retire, building new European-style houses among the ancient granite. From Oumesnat a path leads northwest to the village of **Tamalout**, through the oases and almond orchards of the valley. Wander as far as time allows, as the views become more and more breathtaking – the path to Aït-Taleb takes four hours. In spring the valley is awash with colour when pink and white almond blossom bursts forth among the barren rock.

From Tafraout, either return via Aït-Baha, or continue west to Tiznit (see page 115) and then on the main P30 north to Agadir.

Dra Valley

This drive heads southeast along the ancient camel trail of the Dra valley, through thick palm oases and past crumbling honey-coloured Kasbahs. *The 328km round trip can be accomplished in a day, leaving early from Ouarzazate, lunching in Zagora and returning to Ouarzazate that evening. Alternatively, spend the night in Zagora and amble back to Ouarzazate the following day.*

Make sure you have a good spare tyre and plenty of drinking water. Also ignore people waving you down in the middle of the road – a common hustling ploy.

1 TIZI-N-TINIFIFFT PASS

From Ouarzazate the road passes through scorched plains for 40km as far as the small village of **Aït-Saoun**. Here a dramatic change takes place as you climb 1,680m into the twisted strata of the Jbel Sarhro range. The views back to the Atlas and Ouarzazate are stunning.

64km from Ouarzazate is Agdz, the biggest settlement before Zagora. There is a petrol station here.

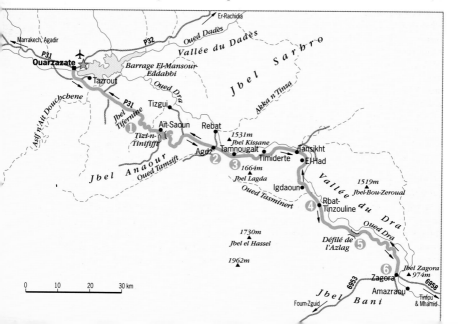

2 AGDZ

Famous for its brightly coloured carpets, Agdz is the old administrative centre for the northern Dra. A kasbah sits on the hill to the east. The Thursday souk is a good place to look for carpets.

From Agdz, the road passes along the Dra river and its lush oases, with ruined kasbahs set against dark cliffs.

3 TAMNOUGALT AND TIMIDERTE

Soon after Agdz are the most impressive *ksour* in the Dra, on the left of the road at Tamnougalt. They are still inhabited by the members of the Berber Mezguita tribe. The kasbah of Timiderte, 8km on, was built by the Glaoui family in 1938.

57km further on is the village of Rbat-Tinzouline.

4 RBAT-TINZOULINE

The largest village in the middle Dra, Rbat-Tinzouline enjoys a dramatic setting against the Jbel-Bou-Zeroual mountains. The Monday souk here is especially lively, with vendors flocking from neighbouring oases. A string of crumbling *ksour* encircle the settlement.

After Rbat-Tinzouline the valley flattens and the oases grow larger. Camels graze the scrubland. This is a big date-producing area and in late October the palms are heavy with ripe fruit.

5 DÉFILÉ DE L'AZLAG (AZLAG GORGE)

The road narrows 25km before Zagora to pass through the Azlag gorge. From the gorge the road leads into the vast oasis of **Ternata** and its countless date palms, home to the Arab tribes of the Oulad Yahia and Roha.

6 ZAGORA

The dusty main street of Zagora seems to come straight from a Wild West frontier town. This is the frontier: the end of modern amenities and the beginning of the *hammada*, the stone desert that leads to the Sahara. A sign at the end of the street proclaims 52 days to Timbuktu from here – by camel. To the south of the town is a conical volcanic hill offering a splendid sunset view over the palm trees. To the southeast, the settlement of Amazraou is a centre for date cultivation.

If you have time, head south to the dunes of Tinfou. Otherwise head back northwest to Ouarzazate.

'The Treasure of the Desert', near Agdz

DRA VALLEY ARCHITECTURE

The architecture of the Dra is remarkable. Fortified towns, or *ksour*, built of baked Saharan earth, rise from the oases like integral parts of the natural surroundings. None is older than 100 years, but all seem timeless, as if carved by spring rains. The entire population of the valley lives in such *ksour*, spending the day talking in the shade of their walls and retreating to their safety at night.

LEGENDS AND SUPERSTITIONS

Silver Fatima hands and magical tattoos

'**S**orcery is burrowing invisible tunnels in every direction, from thousands of senders to thousands of unsuspecting recipients,' wrote Paul Bowles in his autobiography. Moroccans have always believed in mysticism and in rural areas superstitions and sorcerers held as much sway as more orthodox religion. In Berber villages you will still see magic designs painted on doorways as protection from the evil eye. Berber women tattoo their chins with a magical diamond to prevent evil spirits entering the nose and mouth. These spirits, or *jinn*, are said to have been created at the same time as humans, and every human has a *jinn* double. The *jinn* have fluid

Medicine man at jemaa el Fna in Marrakech

bodies and can take any shape, particularly those of household cats and dogs. They inhabit the desert, cemeteries and toilets, which is why, according to legend, you should never go to the lavatory between 11.30pm and 2.30am. Other protections against evil spirits are the 'Fatma' hands seen on doorways or on bracelets and necklaces. A lizard design gives protection against snakes and scorpions. Large triangular designs on Berber bracelets are said to enhance fertility, as do palm tree tattoos on the face and hand (the *siyala*).

Most médinas contain apothecaries, now more tourist attractions than authentic soothsayers. In rural areas traditional cures are still used. Famous remedies include eating the ashes of a crow burnt in a new cooking pot to cure syphilis, and sewing the tail of a cat into your trousers to prevent sea-sickness.

GETTING AWAY FROM IT ALL

The sky, now wholly blue, is of an infinite clearness; we are reminded of those glorious noontides of June at the time of haymaking. No trees anywhere, nothing but these carpets of flowers as far as the view extends...
PIERRE LOTTI
Morocco (1889)

The Deep South

Since peace accords were signed between Morocco and Polisario rebels in 1989, it is safe to visit the Western Sahara. This great expanse of rock, sand and not a lot else is a fascinating glimpse of one of the world's harshest landscapes but offers little in the way of refinement or amenities.

The area comprises four provinces: La'youne, Boujdour, Oued Eddahab (Dakhla) and Smara. La'youne is the capital of the region with a population of 100,000 (compared with 28,000 under Spanish rule up to 1975). The economy of the Western Sahara is traditionally precarious. The Moroccan government has been keen to subsidise the livestock industry – camel meat is successfully exported to the north of the country and neighbouring Arab states. Coastal waters are well-stocked with fish, but there have been difficulties persuading the local Saharawi tribesmen to take to the sea. There is even talk of selling sand from the Sahara to replenish the eroding beaches of the nearby Canary Islands. Tourism is growing, with up-market hotels in La'youne offering desert excursions, excellent sea-fishing and deserted Atlantic beaches. This was Spanish territory until 1975 and the second language is Spanish, although most administrators speak French.

Palm trees and desert kasbahs add to the exotic atmosphere of the South

BIRDWATCHING

Morocco is a key migration route for thousands of birds in spring and autumn, and many resident species provide year-round attractions. White storks, said to be the souls of distant Muslim travellers coming to their summer nests at Allah's bidding, are Morocco's national bird. There are even stork hospitals in Fès and Marrakech. Little egrets dot the countryside, riding on cows' backs, and on the coast puffins and flamingos vie for attention, while in the mountains golden eagles soar alongside Egyptian vultures. Inland, colourful bee-eaters and hoopoe are common winter visitors.

The best viewing grounds are on the coast and at inland lakes. The lakes of the Middle Atlas nourish wading birds, including avocet. On the Atlantic coast Sidi Bourhaba, 25km north of Rabat, is an established bird reserve with an information centre. Further south, Oualidia entertains vast flocks of flamingo, while around Agadir are some of the best waters for waders and even the rare bald ibis.

A white stork, the sacred bird of Morocco

Check the state of your car before heading south – spare tyre, oil and water. Take plenty of drinking water – up to 8 litres a day per person is recommended. Sunglasses and headwear are advisable. Fill up with petrol wherever possible.

GUELMIME TO LA'YOUNE

From Guelmime the P41 runs southwest straight through a series of baked hills. The Dra River, flowing from the High Atlas, rarely makes it this far, especially in recent years of drought, but in Roman times the estuary was infested with crocodiles.

The administrative centre of **Tan-Tan** is a scattering of sandy houses. There is little to see; either head to Tan-Tan Plage, the beach resort 25km west, or continue past into the flat *hammada*.

Further south, sand dunes start to encroach on the road, until you rejoin the sea and a coast of strange cliffs, including an eerie stretch of shipwrecked boats. **Tarfaya** is a good fishing base 234km from Tan-Tan. **La'youne** lies a further 115km south - a breath of civilisation in the desert. This was the target of King Hassan's 1975 Green March (see **History**, page 9) and contains a museum outlining Moroccan developments in the region since then. The old Spanish quarter stands on the hill overlooking a dry riverbed, but La'youne's real attraction is its isolation. Jeep tours will take you into the desert.

Mountain Hiking

Morocco is a country made for hiking. With 400 peaks reaching 3,000m and ten exceeding 4,000m, the Atlas ranges attract numerous hikers of all ages and fitness levels. Even the highest mountain in North Africa, Jbel Toubkal, is feasible for those of average fitness (see page 108). In addition to offering spectacular scenery and good weather conditions, Atlas hiking brings you into contact with mountain Berbers, a proud and hospitable people whose lifestyles have changed little over the centuries. The ideal time to trek in the High Atlas is from May to October, after which snow blocks many paths. In the lower Middle Atlas spring and autumn are the best seasons for walking.

Precautions

Always check on weather conditions, as spring storms and autumn snow are not infrequent. Flash floods in spring can be dangerous, especially in dry river valleys. Make sure you have warm clothing, good boots, and a hat and sunglasses to avoid sunstroke. In the Toubkal Massif, where much of the region is over 3,000m, you might get altitude sickness by ascending too quickly. Headache, dizziness and sickness should be treated with rest – stop at regular intervals and take the ascent slowly. Altitude sickness can kill.

Guides

Taking a guide is an inexpensive way to maximise what you see; mules can be hired to carry baggage.
Contact: Délégation Provinciale de Tourisme, Ifrane (tel: 5 56 60 80). Baadoud Tours Imlil, Poste Asni BP24, Asni, Marrakech (tel: 7 70 03 95 fax; 7 70 75 35). Délégation de Tourisme, place Abdelmoumen, Marrakech (tel: 4 44 88 89, fax: 4 44 89 06).

THE MIDDLE ATLAS

The 250km of the Middle Atlas range are divided into two massifs. To the west, the limestone plateau from Khenifra to Ifrane is a starkly beautiful land of twisted rock formations, oak and cedar forests and small lakes. Organised hiking is possible from the ski-resort of Ifrane, but the real pleasure lies in driving and stopping at will. This is the home of the Barbary apes which roam the cedar forests in large family packs. The best route to take into the cedar forests is the S303 from Khenifra to Ain-Leuh and on along the 3398 to Azrou. Also on this road is the source of Oum er Rbia, Morocco's most important river, 45km north of Khenifra: a series of hot and cold springs bubbles from the cliff. North of Ifrane at Immouzer, a string of small lakes provides fishing and boating facilities.

Further east is the more rugged massif of Taza, including the national park of Tazzeka (see page 140).

Mountain guide

HIGH ATLAS

The High Atlas ranges are dominated by the Toubkal Massif, rising to the south of Marrakech. Easily accessible, this area offers the most dramatic of Morocco's mountains, but is well trodden by tourists (see page 140). Less explored regions include the Azilal Massif to the south of Beni Mellal, where limestone peaks are cut by dramatic gorges. Here are the Cascades d'Ouzoud, waterfalls tumbling from cliffs (see page 98) and the giant reservoir, Bin el Ouidane. Further south, tracks lead high into the remote mountains. This is the summer pasture for nomadic shepherds who bring their flocks to the foothills of the towering Ighil M'Goun range, the second highest in Morocco. This range is also accessible from Ouarzazate.

Furthest east, the Midelt Massif culminates in the majestic 3,747m-high Jbel Ayyachi. Fringed with cedar forests, this epic region provides some of the best and least-known walking, although there is less transport and accommodation. For a direct ascent of Jbel Ayyachi it is best to head to the village of Tattiouine, where trails begin.

Above: gushing waterfalls at Ouzoud
Below: the barren peaks of the High Atlas

Safari

CAMEL TREKKING

In the southern fringes of the Sahara it is possible to take to the 'ship of the desert' and spend time exploring oases and sand dunes by camel. Tours can last from a few hours to several days, with nights spent in the desert under Berber tents. Two main bases for camel treks are in the Ziz Gorge and Dra valley. Merzouga, near Erfoud, where the Erg Chebbi dunes rise 150m and stretch for 15km, is famous for its white camels and Morocco's largest mounds of sand. The *auberges* and restaurants in Merzouga can arrange camel trips. In the Dra valley, Zagora is the main base for camels –

Ships of the desert sail over the sand dunes of Erg Chebbi

from here it used to take gold traders 52 days by camel to Timbuktu. Tours are available from Hôtel Kasbah Asma (BP78 Zagora, tel: (4) 84 72 41, fax: (4) 84 75 27) into the oasis and to the small dunes of Amazraou. Remember to take as much water as you can carry – it is recommended that you consume up to 8–10 litres a day in the desert. Less strenuous camel trips are available on the beaches of Tanger and Agadir.

JEEP TOURS

Rapidly replacing the camel as desert transport, four-wheel drive vehicles are found everywhere in southern Morocco. Many local travel agencies offer jeep tours of the desert areas. Usually you will be in small groups of up to six per vehicle, and the itinerary will be decided by your guide. It is an efficient way to see sights inaccessible by hire car, and often you will eat and lodge with local villagers, providing an interesting insight into traditional life. Alternatively, you can hire your own jeep – the big car hire firms have competitive rates, especially when you hire from your own country. Otherwise there are several specialist companies in Marrakech and Ouarzazate – contact the local tourist offices for details.

MOUNTAIN BIKING

Rapidly expanding as a sport in Morocco, mountain biking is popular in the Middle and High Atlas. In the past daredevils have even ascended Mount Toubkal, with their bikes carried by mules, and then hurtled down precipitous paths 3,000m to Asni. Several overseas companies run more

Land Rovers awaiting their desert breakfasters before setting off to explore the dunes

sedate mountain bike expeditions. Local agencies hiring bikes include:
Atlas Sahara Trek 72 rue de la Liberté, Marrakech (tel: (04) 44 93 50, fax: (04) 44 96 99).
Tourisport 213 avenue Mohammed V, Marrakech (tel: (04) 44 81 39, fax: (04) 44 81 65).
Nomade Cyclo Toursime 11 place du 3 Mars, Ouarzazate (tel: (04) 88 28 40).

MULE TREKKING

For the less daring, an excursion into the mountains by mule is an excellent way to see spectacular countryside and tune in to the pace of life in the Atlas. Mule treks can be arranged in most hill villages. In the High Atlas, Setti-Fatma, Ouirgane, and Imlil are good bases. From Imlil a classic trek heads up to the Aremd horseshoe – a circuit of several hours, returning to Imlil that evening.

From the mule you see Berber villages built into the cliffs, green valley pastures and dramatic, death-defying paths. In the Middle Atlas, Ifrane and Azrou offer mule treks, although these are less well organised. It is better to contact the Tourist Office in Fès for details.
For more serious horseback riding contact **Sport Travel** 8 bis rue Abou Bakr, Marrakech (tel: 43 61 58).

It is important to remember that the Moroccan mountains have only recently opened up to visitors. The environment is fragile and the customs and lifestyle of its population must be respected. Ask before taking photographs, do not hand out sweets, money or pens to local children and take all garbage away with you.

National Parks

TAZZEKA

140km east of Fès, this densely wooded mountain range rises to 1980m. In May and June the forest floor is carpeted with flowers and butterflies appear in abundance.

A spectacular road leads 76km through the park, which is easily accessible on a daytrip from Fès. Take the S311 south from the main P1. The road climbs through the Oued Zireg gorge, winding its way to the Bab Taza pass at 1,540m. Before the pass, a rough track leads 7km north to the summit of Jbel Tazzeka and its TV aerial. Alternatively, footpaths lead to the peak and its grandiose view over verdant hills.

This being limestone country, the park is riddled with subterranean passages. After Bou Idir you descend into the hollow of Daia Chiker and a series of caves, the Grottes du Chiker. North of the road is the park's most

The wooded High Atlas foothills of the Toubkal National Park

famous sight – the **Gouffre de Friouato**. A guide takes you through a 30m cleft in the rock, down 550 rough-hewn steps to a gargantuan 180m-deep cavern. This is said to be the biggest cave system in North Africa, adorned with stalactites. Your guide will attempt to break one off for an extra tip – decline if you can, as these are not growing back as quickly as they are disappearing.

From the Col de Sidi Mejbeur the road descends past the normally dried up Ras-el-Oued waterfalls, through valleys of cherry trees to Taza.

TOUBKAL

Toubkal National Park is the centre for hiking in the High Atlas. It is a wild place of rocky crags, eagles and isolated hill villages. Mount Toubkal, North Africa's highest mountain, is not the only attraction (see page 108) – **Lac d'Ifni**, a serene lake in the cradle of 4,000m peaks, lies just beyond, while east from Imlil the refuge at **Tacheddirt** offers a 3,616m ascent to Jbel Angour.

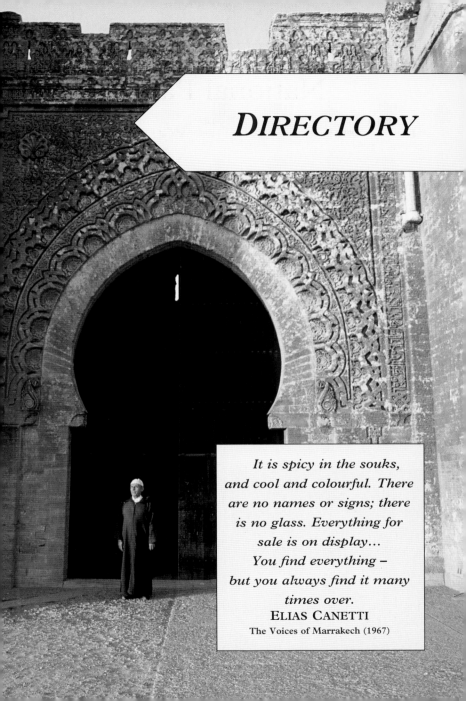

DIRECTORY

> *It is spicy in the souks,*
> *and cool and colourful. There*
> *are no names or signs; there*
> *is no glass. Everything for*
> *sale is on display…*
> *You find everything –*
> *but you always find it many*
> *times over.*
> ELIAS CANETTI
> The Voices of Marrakech (1967)

Shopping

'**C**ome and look, just for the pleasure of the eyes', implore merchants from Tanger to Tiznit. It is difficult to return from Morocco without having bought something; shopping is one of Morocco's most enjoyable pastimes, and after a while the hard sell softens and the bargaining game becomes an entertainment in itself.

While the 'traditional' aspect of many crafts is debatable, their vibrant colours and fine detail will seduce – the Moroccan Government estimates that 20 per cent of your holiday spending will be on handicrafts. You will need to bargain for most items (see **First Steps**). Be firm and do not utter a price you are not prepared to pay. If you shop with guides they will receive a hefty commission, which you inadvertently pay as part of the final price.

Opening hours for most shops are from 8.30am to noon and from 3pm to 7pm. Souks follow a similar pattern, although theoretically they are open continually. Most Moroccans shop between 5pm and 7pm, when streets are liveliest.

Couscous pots in the souks of Marrakech

Antiques
True antiques are rare. Beware of purveyors of ancient gold, silver, daggers, rifles, pots, tables and chests of drawers. In Morocco it is best to stick to freshly crafted goods.

Carpets and *kilim*
Moroccan carpets make colourful and intriguing souvenirs, but more interesting are the Berber *kilim*, woven coverings of the Atlas, with their bright colours and bold geometric designs. The craft museums of Fès and Marrakech contain fine examples. Berber blankets and the red and white striped *ftouh* shawls of the Rif are cheaper. Tetouan has an excellent Berber market.

To get an idea of quality and price it is a good idea to head to the officially run *Centres Artisinal*, where prices are fixed, albeit at higher rates than you should pay in a souk. The Cooperative des Tapis at the Kasbah des Oudayas in Rabat allows visitors to sit in on carpet-knotting.

Each Moroccan carpet is regulated by the state and given a label: blue for superior quality knotting, yellow/orange for good quality and green for average quality.

Jewellery
Moroccan jewellery tends to be bulky and often contrary to western taste. As with carpets, it is best to examine quality and prices in a state-run *Centre Artisinal*

before entering the fray of médina shopping. Berber necklaces and bracelets, made of heavy metal and semi-precious stone, are popular. Tiznit is known for its silverwork.

Leather

Morocco is justly famous for its leather. British aristocracy in the last century sent whole libraries of books to be bound by Moroccan leatherworkers. Today leather jackets have replaced books as the industry's mainstay. Leather *babouches*, or slippers, also make an enduring gift, as do high-quality wallets.

Metalwork

Huge pewter couscous pots and brass dishes seem tempting in a Moroccan setting but often become white elephants in the harsh light of homecoming. More enchanting are the ubiquitous silver spouted teapots, although their durability is minimal.

Pottery

You cannot escape Moroccan pottery. Every roadside has its stall of colourful bowls, plates and urns. Such pottery is inexpensive, highly attractive and looks good in any setting. The road from Rabat to Tanger is an excellent hunting ground. More up-market items are found in Fès.

Spices

Mint is a Moroccan speciality – Meknès is its capital. Saffron is much cheaper in Morocco than elsewhere, and other spices such as cumin, harissa, cinnamon, thyme and ginger abound.

Spice and all things nice at Guelmime market

Apothecaries sell all sorts of weird and wonderful 'natural' make-up, from henna to ghassoul mud for shaving cuts, as well as dubious aphrodisiacs.

Woodwork

The thuya wood craftsmen of Essaouira are among the most talented in the world. This dark, deeply knotted wood is irresistible and boxes, trays, tables, chess sets and wooden cups make excellent gifts.

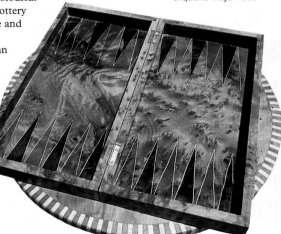

Backgammon board made from Essaouira's exquisite thuya wood

CARPETS

'Moroccan rugs are a poem, a poem that is never the same, that the mind and the hands play with, but that no machine can conceive' – anonymous poem, Meknès carpet shop.

By the time Muslim immigrants from Andalusia introduced Persian knotting techniques to Morocco in the 14th century, Berber tribes had been making carpets for centuries. There are three categories of Moroccan carpet: the Arabic designs and Persian knotting of Rabat, the Berber carpets of the Middle and High Atlas, and *kilim*, thinner rugs which are woven, not knotted.

The techniques of carpet-weaving have changed little over the centuries. In the deep south of Morocco, nomadic tribes still use horizontal looms, carried in rolls and pegged out in the earth at each oasis. Weavers know by heart patterns that are passed down through generations. Larger carpets will be the work of several people, each person working on a 'field' or section. To direct the weaving a master-weaver or *oustad* is appointed to each loom. The *oustad* has an overall idea of the pattern and colours and will often sing out the colours and numbers of

knots, using a different tune for different weavers. This rhythmical song is learned from an early age and legendary *oustads* are said to have 50–60 different designs committed to memory.

In the cities, mechanisation has taken over. Vertical looms are much quicker and designs are copied from patterns.

Rabati carpets are similar to most in the Arab world, with the classic mihrab design in the centre. Colours range between blues, greys and pinks. Although sometimes expensive, such carpets are not good investments, and pale into insignificance beside Turkish and Persian equivalents.

Berber carpets are strikingly distinctive and often unique to a specific tribe. Typically, designs will include strong horizontal lines enclosing diamond and lozenge shapes, believed to have magical properties. Others contain strange animal figures, seemingly ancient mystical symbols but actually a recent adaptation to tourist taste. Such carpets would be used to cover the floors of nomadic tents, or hung to divide the tent into separate 'rooms'.

Moroccan carpets, although not great investments, make vibrant souvenirs

WHERE TO BUY

Before embarking on a bargaining spree in the médina it is always wise to head to a local state-run Centre Artisinal to give you an idea of price and quality. Prices displayed are the maximum you would pay. Many up-market hotels have their own souvenir stalls, and while these are expensive the quality of goods is high, and for the time-pressed they offer an easy alternative to trekking the souks.

THE NORTH

OUJDA
Centre Artisanal
Far from tourist crowds, Oujda offers good-value authentic crafts and is a pleasant place to shop.
Rue el Mouahidine (tel: 68 35 52).

TANGER
Centre Artisanal
For a selection of good-quality craftware at official prices in series of workshops/boutiques.
Avenue de Belgique (tel: 93 31 00).

Galerie Tindouf
A venerable antique shop with a large stock of interesting items.
64 rue de la Liberté, opposite Hotel El Minzah (tel; 93 15 25).

Grand Socco
Lively food market, selling anything from sharks' heads to Riffian blankets.
Place 9 Avril 1947.

Parfumerie Madini
The Madini family have been concocting perfumes for 14 generations. Customers include the Emirs of Kuwait and the late Barbara Hutton.
14 rue Sebou (tel: 93 43 88).

TETOUAN
Souk el Houdz
In the centre of the kasbah – the small Berber market where Riffian women sell colourful blankets and striped *ftouh.*

CENTRAL PLAINS AND MIDDLE ATLAS

AZROU
Coopérative Artisanale
Centre of arts and crafts for the Middle Atlas. Rugs, pottery and wood-carvings.
Place Mohammed V, to the left of the big rock (tel: 56 23 34).

CASABLANCA
Centre 2000
Morocco's one modern shopping mall, with 30 shops and five restaurants.
Boulevard Enphrette Boignet, behind the Port Railway Station.

FÈS
Centre Artisanal
Some of the finest crafts in the country, especially rugs.
Boulevard Allal ben Abdellah, next to the Wilaya de Fès (tel: 62 31 60).

Chez Benlamlih
Top-notch brass and metal work – Benlamlih's father was a craftsman for the royal palace gates in Fès el Jdid.
75 Talâa Kebira (tel: 63 32 35).

English Bookshop of Fès
For any holiday reading needs.
68 avenue Hassan II (tel: 62 08 42).

Maroquinerie Industrielle de Fès
Leather goods direct from the factory at large discounts.
Rue 802 Sidi Brahim Industrial Zone (tel: 64 19 41).

Palais de Fès
Large carpet selection, good mint tea and a view over the Karaouiyne Mosque.
16 Boutouil Karaouiyne (tel: 63 73 05).

MEKNÈS
L'Artisinat de l'Or
Well-stocked bazaar, including Meknès embroidery and Berber carpets.
10 Sahat Moulay Ismail (tel: 53 03 13).

RABAT
Centre Artisanal
Workshops on two levels, with good-value goods and a currency exchange.
6 rue Tariq al Marsa (below the Oudayas Kasbah). No telephone.

Rue des Consuls
One street in the northeast corner of the médina – the best place in the country for an Arab-style knotted carpet.

THE SOUTH

ESSAOUIRA
Galerie Mogador
Young designer Abdennasser Boumazzourh's immaculate desks,

wardrobes and bracelets are much sought after in Paris and Milan.
3 rue du Yemen (tel: 47 24 94).

MARRAKECH
Centre Artisanal
Impressive rugs, pottery and metalwork.
Avenue Mohammed V (tel: 44 36 64).

La Porte d'Or
One of the better carpet shops, with helpful, friendly staff.
115 rue Souk Smarine (tel: 44 54 54).

OUARZAZATE
Ensemble Artisanal
One of the best in the country, with stonework, copper and Berber *kilim* and rugs at competitive prices.
Boulevard Mohammed V, in front of the kasbah (tel: 88 24 92).

TAMGROUT
Coopérative Poterie de Tamegroute
A small pottery cooperative, where the clay is fired in medieval ovens and glazed with dark green Tamegroute colouring.
Route P31 Tamgrout. No telephone.

A street vendor in the Medina, Fès

SOUKS (MARKETS)
In the country

Morocco is a country of markets in which everyone has something to sell. In the countryside farmers often set off at dawn, arriving at the souk soon after daybreak to shop, gossip and shop some more. On such days roads are blocked with donkeys, cafés are packed, and the town is alive with noise and bustle. Come dusk the exodus begins. The next day the town is quiet once more, waiting for the following week.

Many towns and villages are actually named after their souk day, an indication of how important the market is. For example, Souk el Arba, between Rabat and Tanger, has its souk on a Wednesday:

el Had Sunday
el Tnine Monday
el Tleta Tuesday
el Arba Wednesday
el Khemis Thursday
el Jemaa Friday (usually no market because it is the holy day)
el Sebt Saturday

Urban souks

In the heart of the médina, the link between shopping and religion is close – the wealthiest shops are found closest to the mosque, serving pilgrims and often paying rent to the mosque for use of their premises.

FÈS
Attarine souk

Laden with spices, from turmeric and coriander to priceless saffron and musk. Alongside are smaller souks dealing in gold and jewellery.

Cherabliyin souk

Halfway along Talaa Kebira, this is the slipper-makers' souk, where babouches are made (Fassi slippers are the best in Morocco).

Kissaria

The fabric souk, a modern market replacing the old souk burnt down by French authorities in 1954, is lively,

Henna for sale in the souks of Fès

although without much charm. Enjoy the rows of immaculate silk and colourful slippers.

Souk des Teinturiers
The dyers' souk (Souk Sabbighin in Arabic) is a surreal place, where bright bundles of wool hang to dry against blackened walls (see pages 82–3).

Souk el Henna
Just off Souk Attarine is one of the most popular souks – stalls of henna, natural make-up, strange spices, and, so the stallholders claim, aphrodisiacs. In one corner, a palatial rug shop was once the médina's madhouse.

Tanneries
The tanneries – vats of multicoloured liquid, bare-footed men, the stench of dead skins – are Fès' most memorable sight, and the furthest removed from modernday life (see page 83).

MARRAKECH
Leading northwards from the Jemaa el Fna the souks are as follows:

Souk Smarine
Beginning with stalls of pottery and spices, including technicolour displays of olives, Souk Smarine then leads north, past dozens of textile stalls selling bright kaftans.

Rhaba Kedima and Criée Berbère
Rhaba Kedima is a distinctive square filled with apothecary stalls and street vendors. Once the grain market, it now houses dried snakes, skins, and chickens. Opposite, a small passage leads to the Criée Berbère, a small square used for carpet auctions – the famed 'Berber market' touted by guides.

Souk Attarin and Souk des Teinturiers
Souk Attarin at the heart of the médina, traditionally the perfume souk, is now dominated by western clothes. To the west lies the famous Souk des Teinturiers where blackened dyers hang out their psychedelic bundles of wool. Just north is Souk Chouari, home to basket-weavers and wood-carvers, and Souk Haddadine, a jumbled confusion of iron, where you are serenaded by beating hammers.

Souk Cherratin
North of the Kissaria is Souk Cherratin, the leather souk, which has lost much of its traditional attraction. This is where books were bound, purses sewn and sandals made. Today there are increasing numbers of tourist boutiques.

SPECIALITIES OF OTHER TOWNS
Azrou carpets, carved wood
Essaouira wood craft, spices
Meknès mint, slippers, embroidery
Midelt carpets
Ouarzazate carpets
Taroudannt stone carving, silver, animal furs
Tetouan Berber blankets, instruments
Tiznit silver jewellery
Rabat carpets
Salé pottery

Entitlement

*T*he most common form of entertainment in Morocco is to sip mint tea and watch the world go by. Throughout the country you will see cafés full of men drinking, chatting and smoking (women are conspicuous by their absence). It is said that more Moroccan business is done in the café than the office.

Nightlife tends to be in up-market hotels, although some nightclubs put on shows of belly-dancing and folklore. But barely a month goes by without some major festival, celebrating local saints or successful harvests. And there is always the world's greatest street fair – the Jemaa el Fna of Marrakech.

BARS

It is not difficult to find a drink in Morocco. Outside major hotels most bars tend to be all-male affairs.

AGADIR
Corniche Restaurant Bar and Jour et Nuit
Two lively beachfront bars. The former has live music from local bands.

CASABLANCA
Diplomat Bar
Plush décor, jazz and luxury.
Hotel El Mansour, 27 avenue des FAR (tel: 31 30 11).

FÈS
Jazz Bar
Luxury and style. Jazz most nights.
Hotel Jnan Palace, avenue Ahmed Chaouki (tel: 65 39 65).

MARRAKECH
Le Churchill Piano Bar
Gentlemen's club feel; jazz piano.
La Mamounia Hotel, avenue Bab Jdid (tel: 44 89 81).

MEKNÈS
Hotel Transatlantique
View from the terrace over the médina.
Hotel Transatlantique, rue El Meriniyine (tel: 52 00 02).

The Rif
Meknès' most happening place.
Hotel Rif, rue d'Accra (tel: 52 25 91).

Les Ambassadeurs, Negociants, Le Regent
Male-dominated bars.
6, 108, 34 boulevard Mohammed V (no telephone).

Renaissance
Stunning view from the 9th-floor terrace.
87 avenue Mohammed V (no telephone).

RABAT
Balima Bar
The place for a beer. Crowded terrace.
Hotel Balima, 173 avenue Mohammed V (tel: 70 86 25).

TANGER
Caid's Bar
In the El Minzah hotel. Elegant décor opening onto gardens and pool.
Hotel El Minzah, 85 rue de la Liberté (tel: 93 58 85).

Emma's BBC
Plastic tablecloths on the beach. BBC stands for Beach Bar Carousel.
Avenue des FAR (no telephone).

Traditional dance and music are features of many Moroccan nightclubs

Tangerinn
Ex-pat bar, crowded pub atmosphere.
1 rue Magellan (tel: 93 53 37).

The Pub
Food, beer and British pub décor.
4 rue Sorolla (tel: 93 47 89).

La Fontaine
Casa's most infamous strip club.
Boulevard Mohammed el Hansali (no telephone).

Rick's Bar
Imitation *Casablanca* bar, complete with bogus Bogarts and a piano.
Hyatt Regency Hotel, place des Nations Unies (tel: 26 12 34).

CABARET AND FANTASIAS
Many hotels run folklore evenings, combining belly-dancing (*shikat*) with traditional dancing and singing. In tourist centres large venues are used for fantasias, re-enactments of Berber cavalry charges with dancing and food. Most can be booked through your hotel .

AGADIR
All the beachfront hotels have cabarets; the best are the Sahara and the Atlas.

CASABLANCA
Holiday Inn
Belly-dancing 15 storeys up.
Holiday Inn Crowne Plaza, Rond Point Hassan II (tel: 29 49 49).

FÈS
Al Firdaous
Folk spectacle with dinner each evening from 9pm in a converted palace.
10 rue Zenifour near Hotel Palais Jamai (tel: 63 43 43).

MARRAKECH
Ancien Casino de Marrakech
No gambling, but belly-dancing, swordplay and snakes.
Hotel es Saadi, avenue el Kadissia (tel: 44 88 11).

TANGER
Morocco Palace
Belly-dancing till 1am, then a disco.
Rue Prince Moulay Abdullah (tel: 93 86 14).

CINEMAS

Most Moroccan towns possess at least one cinema, offering a regular diet of Kung Fu and Indian love stories. Most films are dubbed into French – English versions are rare.

HAMMAM

Every district of the médina has its own public bath, or *hammam*. In most there are separate bathing hours for men and women, usually 9am–5pm for women, 5pm–midnight for men. In some towns there may be separate single-sex *hammam*. Mixed bathing is not permitted: indeed, in the past a man entering a woman's *hammam* would be executed on the spot.

Washing is an integral part of Islamic worship. Each mosque contains a fountain and ablutions pool where the faithful must wash their hands, arms, face and feet before prayer. After sexual intercourse it is necessary to wash seven times. As the Prophet Muhammad said, 'Cleanliness is next to Godliness'. Yet for many Moroccans a trip to the local *hammam* is more than religious observance – it is a chance to meet friends, chat and relax. For a visitor it provides an enjoyable insight into a popular bathing culture long since vanished in the west.

The water is hot. In a basic *hammam* you douse yourself liberally with buckets of water; larger *hammams* have several pools, each of varying temperatures, in which you wallow. Massages are also offered, although these are sometimes not for the faint-hearted.

A women's *hammam* is one of the few places where Western women can meet Moroccan women. Here, away from the male-dominated streets, the atmosphere is relaxed and friendly.

NIGHTCLUBS

AGADIR
Disco Tan Tan
Lively hotel disco.
Hotel Les Almohades, boulevard du 20 Août (tel: 84 02 33).

Le Byblos
High-tech disco.
Hotel Dunes D'Or, Cité Balnéaire (tel: 84 01 50).

CASABLANCA
Le Calypso
International beachfront disco.
Ain Diab (tel: 93 67 15).

MARRAKECH
Le Club
Exclusive dancing in the bowels of La Mamounia hotel.
Hotel La Mamounia, avenue Bab Jdid (tel: 44 89 81).

TANGER
Borsalino's
Smart mainstream disco.
Rue Prince Moulay Abdullah.

Up 2000
Top-floor dancing in a silver flying saucer.
Hotel Les Almohades, avenue des FAR (tel: 94 04 31).

SPAS

The curative waters of Morocco have been enjoyed and exploited ever since Roman times. In the Middle Atlas, water rich in minerals springs forth from volcanic rock at a steady 54°C. Moulay Yacoub, just outside Fès, is an ultra-modern thermal station amidst the rolling Trhrat hills.

Opened in 1992, this luxurious complex comprises hot water swimming pools, individual mineral baths, massage relaxation and beauty treatment, as well as four specialised medical departments. A week's intensive health treatment is inexpensive by western standards, with accommodation at the neighbouring Motel de Moulay Yacoub. There are also more old-fashioned spa baths at Sidi Harazem, 15km east of Fès.

Thermes de Moulay Yacoub, 20km northwest of Fès (tel: 69 40 66). Accommodation from Hotel Moulay Yacoub, Moulay Yacoub Autonomous Centre (tel: 69 40 35, fax: 69 40 12).

SOUND AND LIGHT SHOWS

FÈS
Borj Sud is site of a new 600-seat *Son et Lumière* show, during summer months (contact the Tourist Office for details).

STREET ENTERTAINMENT

From the cantankerous old watersellers in Casablanca to the excitable snake-charmers of Marrakech and the Andalusian musicians of Tetouan, Morocco provides a memorable selection of informal entertainment. The capital of street entertainment is undoubtedly the Jemaa el Fna. Here, black cobras dance and trained monkeys jump among Tazeroualt acrobats. Few spectacles rival the scene at sunset, with smoke billowing from food grills and dancers, boxers, storytellers, drummers, orange juice vendors and serpent charmers all vying for the attention of the massed crowds.

A chleuh dancer gives his all in Jemaa el Fna, Marrakech

MUSIC AND

'The whole Muslim world is practically controlled by music', noted William S Burroughs. Everywhere you go in Morocco you will hear music playing, as it has for countless centuries.

Traditionally, there are two sorts of Moroccan music: the simple oral poetry of the countryside, and sophisticated instrumental music which originated in Andalusia over 1,000 years ago. Andalusian music is Morocco's classical music and is usually played by large orchestras – violins, lutes, tambourine and even the odd piano. This style is the most commonly recorded, and you will hear it everywhere. Its haunting harmonies, often a single theme repeating, tell of lost love and passionate betrothal.

Country music is a collective music, involving numerous musicians, storytellers and dancers. In the High

Atlas, the Berber tribes gather on festive occasions to dance to a simple pipe (*nai*) and drums (*bendirs*), forming a large circle into which pass selected

DANCE

traditionally used to dispel evil spirits. This animated southern music tells of religious, social and worldly themes, exalting love and the joys of drinking.

The most famous of Moroccan dances is the *guedra*, performed by tribeswomen of the Sahara. This traditional erotic dance, in which women crouch low, gyrating their hips as a hint to the male audience, gradually removing layers of veils, is commonly held for tour groups in Agadir hotels (without its traditional finale, when the last garment is removed).

While older musical traditions are strictly upheld, there has been a recent turn towards synthesised music from

Music and dance are everywhere in Morocco, from country fields to bustling medinas

storytellers. More specialised *Chleuh* dances are traditionally a sexual invitation to onlookers, performed by young boys.

Further south, the influence of African rhythms is evident: in the music of the *gnaoua* brotherhood the long-necked gimbri pipe accompanies *garagab* (castanets) to create a rhythmic chant,

Algeria – Rai. This 'North African Rap' is the music of the young, and its heavy beat and harsh electric guitar can be heard in most médina.

Festivals

Moroccan festivals (*moussem*) are generally religious in inspiration. Annual pilgrimages are made to the tombs of local saints, accompanied by music and dancing. Celebrations may last for several days, when quiet country towns are transformed into encampments of tents, itinerant food stalls, entertainers and herds of horses. Local harvests are celebrated in similar fashion.

Several Moroccan festivals have an international reputation. These include the summer arts festival in Asilah; the June folk festival in Marrakech, in which performers from every region of Morocco descend on the ruined El Badi palace – it's worth planning an entire trip around it; and the autumn fantasia in Meknès – the most impressive in the country. The dates of many festivals vary each year, in accordance with the Muslim calendar. Contact local Tourist Offices for information.

At any religious festival discretion is required when taking photographs.

A ritual meeting at the rose festival of El-Kelaa-M'Gouna

Principal Festivals

February Almond blossom festival, Tafraout.

March Theatre festival, Casablanca; cotton festival, Beni Mellal.

May Rose festival, El-Kelaa-M'Gouna.

June Folk festival in the El Badi palace, Marrakech; cherry festival, Sefrou; *moussem* at Asni near Marrakech, Saharan *moussem* at Tan-Tan; camel festival, Asrir, near Guelmime.

July Honey festival, Immouzer Ida Ouatanan; water festival, Martil near Tetouan.

August International Arts Festival, Asilah; *moussem* of Setti-Fatma, Ourika near Marrakech; *moussem* of Sidi Allal Al Hadh, Chechaouen; *moussem* of Moulay

An explosive start to the Fantasia of Meknès

Abdessalem, including fantasia, near El Jadida; festival of African music, Tiznit; Apple festival, Immouzer du Kandar.

September Fantasia in Meknès, one of the biggest festivals in Morocco; traditional arts festival, Fès; *moussem* of Moulay Idriss II, when Fassi craftsmen sacrifice cattle in honour of the city's patron saint; *moussem* of Sidi Ahmed Ou Moussa, Agadir; marriage festival, Imilchil; *moussem* of Moulay Idriss I, Moulay Idriss.

October Date festival, Erfoud; music festival, Essaouira.

December Olive festival, Rhafsaï, in the Rif.

WEDDINGS

Moroccan marriages are times of collective celebration, when whole towns join in the rituals that precede the wedding. Traditionally, the father selects a bride for his son. The son has an opportunity to see the chosen girl, at a distance, to express his opinion. All being well, the father then offers the bride's family a dowry. If accepted, this leads to an engagement of one to two years. The engagement is a legal part of the marriage process, committing the couple to each other, and as such permits them to sleep with each other if they so wish.

An urban wedding between wealthy families might last a week, with each day designated for a different ritual. In poorer, rural areas, the wedding often lasts a single day. Before the wedding, there are still numerous rituals that must be followed. . After the allotted period of preparation the bride is carried to the bridegroom's house, together with music, dancing and general uproar. She enters the bridal chamber and the guests settle down to a large meal with further music and dancing. In traditional Berber weddings, the bride is brought to the bridegroom's house on a horse, and then hidden in an upstairs room curtained with carpets so only close family may peek in. The bridegroom must ascend a wooden ladder to reach her.

As in all domains of Moroccan life, the marriage process has been changing rapidly. In cities women now have as much say in the choice of their partner as their western counterparts. Dowries are no longer an issue: dual incomes, mortgages and tax benefits are more important considerations than gold or camels.

Children

*B*ringing children to Morocco may not seem like the best idea for a relaxing holiday, but it is a country which welcomes children with endless natural playgrounds, fairytale cities and excellent beaches. Moroccan society is firmly based on the family unit and children are greeted with great enthusiasm.

Make sure that children are well covered, wearing hats, sunglasses and loose fitting clothes, and are kept out of the sun. Apart from these simple precautions there is little to worry about – a Moroccan holiday will be an unforgettable experience for any child.

Most families tend to base themselves in one of Morocco's coastal resorts, venturing into the cities for day trips. The Mediterranean coast is a popular destination, with resorts like Kabila and Smir-Restinga tailoring their facilities specifically for families. For slightly older children, hiring a car and seeing some of the countryside is always memorable. In the cities busy médinas can be overwhelming for small children, but fascinating for older age-groups. Ruins such as Chellah and Kasbah des Oudayas in Rabat or the El Badi palace in Marrakech provide eternal inspiration for children's games.

BABIES

Moroccan pharmacies are very well stocked. Medical services in urban areas are highly competent. The usual brands of disposable nappies are available, as are baby food and most common medicines. All pharmacists speak French; fewer speak English.

BEACHES

The best beaches for young children are on the Mediterranean coast from Ceuta to Al-Hoceima, where sheltered bays provide excellent swimming. The new resort of Marinasmir has been developed for families, with baby-sitting facilities, playgrounds and 3km of sand. There is also a large aqua park. On the Atlantic coast, offshore currents are strong and swimming is dangerous. Sheltered beaches include Temara, Skhirat, Oualidia and Agadir. The beach clubs of Aïn Diab on the Casablanca corniche are well suited to children, with sports facilities, swimming pools and restaurants.

CAMELS AND MULES

Camel rides are always popular with children. During the summer season camels patrol the beaches of Tangier, Martil and Agadir. In the Middle and High Atlas mules can be hired for short treks into the hills (see page 139). In Marrakech horse-drawn *calèches* are a good way to see the city with children; they can be hired per hour or per journey.

CAVES

East of Fès, the Friouato cave in the Tazzeka National Park provides an interesting diversion – children enjoy finding the impressive collection of stalactites (see page 140). With a guide the cave is perfectly safe. Elsewhere, the Grotte du Chameau near Oujda (see page 42) is less well organised, but with a flashlight you should be able to find the famous camel-shaped stalactite.

THE DESERT

The Dra and Ziz valleys are ideally suited to children, with exotic kasbahs to play in, palm tree oases to explore and the lure of desert sand dunes at Tinfou and Erfoud. Swimming should not be attempted in southern rivers – many are infected with bilharzia.

GARDENS

The gardens of Marrakech are always popular with kids (see page 94) – the Menara gardens and pool, the Aguedal basin, and particularly the Majorelle gardens provide endless inspiration for games. In Rabat the Chellah and Oudayas gardens are equally entertaining.

HEALTH

Moroccan pharmacies are very well stocked and medical attention is more than competent. Take necessary precautions such as keeping children's heads well covered against the sun, drinking only bottled water and avoiding raw fruit and vegetables that may be washed in contaminated water. Health risks in tourist resorts are minimal.

SAFARI

One of the highlights of Morocco for any child is a daytrip in the Middle Atlas to see wild monkeys. The drive from Azrou to Khenifra is best suited for a monkey safari (see page 136). On the coast, large flocks of flamingos are also star attractions – try the Lac de Sidi Bourhaba just north of Rabat, Oualidia, and Oued Sous outside Agadir.

School children in Ouezzane

Sport

*D*espite extreme temperatures and landscapes, Moroccans are active and passionate sportspeople. Football is the national addiction, while King Hassan's predilection for golf has led to the construction of world-class courses; and the varied topography offers endless possibilities for more adventurous pursuits.

BALLOONING

In the summer two French balloonists run trips over Marrakech and further south towards the desert.
Montgolfières Sud, Marrakech (tel: 44 61 80).

FISHING

Morocco is blessed with a refreshing amount of water and fishing is plentiful. Coarse fishing is most popular, with lakes and reservoirs well stocked with bass, perch and pike. Try the string of lakes east of Immouzer Kandar, Moulay Youssef, east of Marrakech, and El Kansera, west of Meknès. Permits are required: information from *Administration des Eaux et Forêts, 11 rue Revoil, Rabat (tel: 72 53 35).* Bring your own equipment.

Sea-fishing requires no permit and the Atlantic coastal waters are ideal for surfcasting – mackerel, bream, sea bass and tuna are the main attractions. The sea off the Western Sahara provides some of the best game fishing in the world. For information contact Best of Morocco, Seend Park, Seend, Melksham, Wiltshire, SM12 6NZ, England (tel: 01380 828533 or fax: 01380 828630) or Sochatour, 72 boulevard Zerktouni, Casablanca, Morocco (tel: 22 75 13).

FOOTBALL

Morocco is one of the rising stars of world soccer, the national team having qualified for both the 1986 and 1994 World Cup finals. Everywhere you go you will see football matches, from High Atlas hill villages to the beaches of Casablanca. Moroccan playing style is characterised by skilful close control and passing reminiscent of South American football. Matches take place on Sundays.

GOLF

In a land touched by the Sahara there is no shortage of bunkers, but it may come as a surprise to find lush greens and immaculate fairways. Morocco is rapidly becoming a top golfing destination, offering 14 courses. King Hassan II is a golf fanatic, and under his patronage once barren landscapes have blossomed into golfing oases. Green charges are lower than in Europe and the weather is consistently good, attracting ardent amateurs from all over the world. The top professionals gather each year at the Royal Dar Es Salam near Rabat for the King Hassan II trophy.

Agadir
Les Dunes (tel: 83 46 90).
Royal Golf D'Agadir (tel: 24 12 78).
Ben Slimane (near Casablanca)
Royal Golf Club (tel: 32 87 93).
Cabo Negro (near Tetouan)
Cabo Negro Royal Golf Club (tel: 97 83 03).
Casablanca
Anfa Royal Golf Club (tel: 36 10 26).
El-Jadida (south of Casablanca)
Royal Golf Club (tel: 35 22 51).
Fès
Royal Golf, route d'Immouzer (tel: 76 38 49).

That sinking feeling at Rabat's Royal Dar Es Salam golf course

Marrakech
Palmeraie (tel: 30 20 45).
Royal Golf (tel: 44 43 41).
Meknès
Royal Golf, El Mancha (tel: 53 07 53).
Mohammedia
Royal Golf (tel: 32 46 56).
Ouarzazate
Royal Golf Club (tel: 58 26 53).
Rabat
Royal Dar Es Salam (tel: 75 58 64).
Tanger
Royal Golf Club (tel: 94 44 84).

HIKING AND CLIMBING

The Middle and High Atlas, Anti-Atlas and Rif ranges provide numerous hiking possibilities for all levels of fitness (see page 136). Local agencies specialising in hiking include Atlas Tours, *72 rue de la Liberté, Marrakech (tel: 43 38 58)*, and Ribat Tours, *3 avenue Moulay Youssef, Rabat (tel: 70 03 95)*.

The High Atlas also provide numerous climbing regions, notably the Imlil and El Kelaa des M'Gouna regions. For further information contact the Club Alpin Français, *BP 6178 Casablanca (tel: 27 00 90, fax: 29 72 92)*.

HUNTING

Hunting has a tradition in Morocco that goes back to Roman days when Berber warriors were sent out to catch lions, leopards and elephants for Roman amphitheatres. Morocco's present hunting reserves offer grouse and fowl as well as wild boar.

Estates are often owned by travel groups – Sochatour, at *72 boulevard Zerktouni, Casablanca (tel: 27 75 13)*, is the biggest, with reserves near Marrakech, Agadir and Tanger. They will also arrange temporary import licences for guns.

RIDING

Arab horses are justly famous for their grace, speed and volatile temper. Morocco offers exhilarating riding, from the foothills of the High Atlas to the plains of Meknès. The recognised base for mountain riding holidays is La Roseraie at Ouirgane, 60km south of Marrakech (tel: 43 20 94). On the Mediterranean coast, Cabo Negro provides riding holidays at La Ferma (tel: 97 80 75). For general information contact the *Fédération Royale de Sports Equestres, Dar Salam BP 742, Rabat (tel: 75 44 24)*.

RUNNING

Jogging is a serious sport in Morocco, where personal fitness is a matter of pride to every young male. Moroccan middle and long distance runners compete with the best in the world –

Skiing Moroccan style at Oukaïmeden, one of the world's highest ski lifts

Khalid Skah won an Olympic 10,000m gold medal in the 1992 Barcelona Olympics. Along with football, running is seen as a path to untold riches; Skah has been rewarded with property, money and businesses in his home country.

Moroccan women rarely take part in sporting activity, but foreign female joggers seem to be treated with great respect – much more so than when they are mere walkers through crowded médinas.

SKIING

Oukaïmeden, 75km south of Marrakech, is the top skiing resort, open from December until April. It has one of the world's highest lifts (over 3,000m), and offers seven runs, plus hotels and ski hire. Morocco's second resort, Mischliffen, in the Middle Atlas, is less reliable – its three main runs are open for about six weeks each winter. Off-piste skiing is becoming very popular in the High Atlas, with skiers hiking to remote

Watersports are well catered for in Morocco, particularly around Agadir in the South

4000m summits with their skis on mules, and hurtling down virgin pistes. This is recommended for only the most experienced skier.

There are no ski hotlines in Morocco. For information contact the Fédération Royale Marocaine de Ski et Montagne, *Parc de la Ligue Arabe, BP 15 899 Casablanca (tel: 20 37 98)*, or the Club de Ski, *boulevard Mohammed V, Marrakech, (tel: 43 40 26)*.

TENNIS

With all-year-round good weather, Morocco is a tennis-player's paradise. Most big hotels now have their own courts, usually clay. Agadir is the kingdom's tennis capital, boasting over 130 courts. Most courts are floodlit for night play, when temperatures are more bearable. Equipment can be hired from hotels but it is preferable to bring your own racquet and balls.

WATERSPORTS

With 3,530km of coastline, there is much potential for messing about in Moroccan water. The only drawback is the strong off-shore current along the Atlantic coast – it is best to stick to resorts mentioned in the What to See section. Agadir is the centre of aquatic action, offering water skiing, jet-ski, sub-aqua diving, pedalos and even paragliding. Further north, Essaouira is known as Wind City Afrika to legions of top-class surfers. International windsurf competitions are held here each spring. Other top surfing venues include Taghazout, near Agadir, Plage des Nations, at Rabat, and Mehdia. The Mediterranean coast is much calmer and better suited to more sedate aquatic sport: M'Diq has a Yachting Club that arranges sailing courses in the summer (tel: 97 76 94).

Inland, the rivers of the High Atlas are becoming famous for canoeing and white water rafting. 'Tubing' in which you tumble along rapids in a rubber tube, is also popular. For information, contact the *Fédération Royale Marocaine de Canoë-Kayak, Centre National des Sports BP 332, avenue Ibnou Sina, Rabat (tel: 77 88 95)*.

Most small towns have inexpensive municipal swimming pools. Further south, pools are restricted to up-market hotels, which usually permit non-residents to swim for a small fee or if you buy drinks or food.

Food and Drink

*N*ourished by African sunshine, spiced by Arab ingenuity and refined by French subtlety, Moroccan cuisine is among the best in the world. Most Moroccans eat at home, the evening meal being the most important. A genuine invitation to share a Moroccan family meal should not be turned down – this is where you will taste the national cuisine at its best. Outside the home, a whole range of restaurants welcomes the visitor, from the grill stands of the Jemaa el Fna to the exclusive French restaurants of Casablanca and Rabat.

Fast food at Aïn Diab, Casablanca

Gourmet palaces to street stalls

At the top end of the market, traditional Moroccan cuisine is served with Western-style efficiency. In many cities, old palaces have been converted into sumptuous dining rooms. Small local restaurants offer the same traditional food at lower prices, often in similarly authentic surroundings.

On the street, numerous makeshift grills serve tender mutton, grilled fish, fresh salads, thick *harira* soup and hunks of bread. You should go easy on your stomach at first, but you will soon adapt to this most Moroccan of culinary feasts.

Remember that in smaller towns, restaurants will shut from sunrise to sunset during Ramadan.

Prices

You can eat very cheaply in Morocco, and most meals will cost below 100DH. Top restaurants can charge three times this amount. The following restaurants are listed under four price headings, indicating cost per person excluding alcohol. In most establishments a government tax of between 17 and 19 per cent is included; 10 per cent service tax is sometimes included but is usually at the discretion of the client.

D   Cheap
DD   Moderate
DDD   Expensive
DDDD   Very expensive

THE NORTH

ASILAH
La Alkasaba DD
Once run by Lord Churchill, this seafront restaurant specialises in seafood. *Place Zallach (tel: 91 70 12)*.

CHECHAOUEN
Restaurant Tissemlal Casa Hassan D
Delicious good value food in a converted palace. Also an inexpensive bed and breakfast. *22 rue Targui (tel: 98 61 53)*.

TANGER
El Korsan DDD
The best Moroccan restaurant in town,

in the immaculate El Minzah hotel. *Hotel El Minzah, rue de la Liberté (tel: 93 58 85).*

Guitta's DDD
Famous in the international era, this is still one of the best and most select restaurants in the city. European cuisine. *Avenue Sidi Mohammed Ben Abdallah (tel: 93 73 33).*

La Grenouille DD
Just off boulevard Pasteur, a 1950s atmosphere and good European-style food. *3 rue Rembrandt (tel: 93 62 42).*

Restaurant Africa D
Friendly welcome and simple tasty Moroccan dishes opposite the train station. *83 rue Salaha Eddine El Ayoubi (tel: 93 54 36).*

San Remo DD
A small Italian restaurant serving good home-made pasta and pizza. *15 rue Ahmed Chaouki (tel: 93 84 51).*

TETOUAN
Kabila DD
Poolside restaurant offering fish and European specialities. *10km north of Tetouan on the P28 (tel: 97 50 13).*

CENTRAL PLAINS AND MIDDLE ATLAS

CASABLANCA
A Ma Bretagne DDDD
This is Morocco's most famous French restaurant, serving a dazzling array of fish and seafood. The high standard of the kitchens is matched by the price of the food. *Ain Diab, boulevard Sidi Abderrahmane (tel: 36 21 12).*

Al Mounia DDD
Set in a small garden by an ancient dragon tree, with excellent Moroccan specialities. *95 rue Prince Moulay Abdallah (tel: 22 26 69).*

Restaurant de l'Etoile Marocain D
Excellent value for good Moroccan dishes in a traditional setting. *107 rue Alla Ben Abdallah, behind the market (tel: 31 41 00).*

Sakura DDD
Morocco's first and only Japanese restaurant, in immaculate surroundings. *Sheraton Hotel, 100 avenue des FAR (tel: 31 78 78).*

Kebabs sizzling in the Jemaa el Fna, Marrakech

MOROCCAN FOOD

Moroccan cuisine is renowned worldwide for its simple yet delicious recipes: succulent meat dishes, rich pastries and exotic fruits. French master-chef Robert Carrier has even written his own book of Moroccan favourites. To experience the delights of a cuisine that is rivalled only by Turkey in the Arab world, it is necessary to go beyond the precincts of the big hotels and seek out local traditional restaurants.

A traditional meal might start with *harira*, a thick spiced soup of vegetables and meat, commonly eaten to break the fast each sunset during Ramadan. Your waiter will whisper *bismillah* – 'in the name of God' as a sign for you to begin.

Next would come *mechoui*, the most impressive of Moroccan dishes – a whole lamb, roasted in clay ovens. In most restaurants *mechoui* must be ordered in advance. You tear off pieces of tender meat (always with your right hand only – the left is reserved for more basic functions) and eat them with round *khobza* bread.

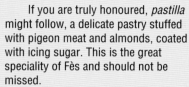

If you are truly honoured, *pastilla* might follow, a delicate pastry stuffed with pigeon meat and almonds, coated with icing sugar. This is the great speciality of Fès and should not be missed.

The main course will be either *tajine* or *couscous*, Morocco's national dishes. *Tajine* is a meat or fish stew, delicately flavoured with olives. *Couscous* is served as the traditional Friday meal in the home: mountains of semolina served with stewed vegetables and mutton. In the south, *couscous* is cooked with onions and raisins, meat and vegetables being rare commodities. Traditionally *couscous* is eaten with the right hand, rolling the grains into a ball and dipping them into the sauce.

To finish this gastronomic feast, *cornes de gazelles* pastries are the most famous dessert – small crescents stuffed with almonds and honey, washed down with *thé à la menthe*.

Harira – thick spiced soup eaten at Ramadan

Pastilla (right) and
Mechoui roast (below)

A traditional banquet
of couscous

Dining in style at the Dar Saada restaurant in Fès

FÈS
Al Fassia DDDD
World-renowned Fassi cuisine in elegant surroundings. Nightly floorshow. *Hotel Palais Jamai Bab Guissa (tel: 63 43 31).*

Dar Saada DDD
A converted palace serving good Moroccan food (lunch only). *21 Souk Attarine (tel: 63 33 43).*

L'Herbier de l'Atlas DDDD
One of the best restaurants in Fès. Music and floorshow. *Hotel Jnan Palace, avenue Ahmed Chaouki (tel: 65 39 65).*

Le Palais de Fès DD
A converted médina palace, overlooking the Karaouiyne Mosque. *16 Boutouil Karaouiyne (tel: 63 73 05).*

MIDDLE ATLAS
Chalet du Lac D
A French hunting lodge on Lake Aowa, serving European specialities and good wine. *Imouzzer du Kandar, Dayet Aou (tel: 66 32 70).*

RABAT
Goëland DDD
Relaxed French restaurant, a favourite with the diplomatic community. *Open noon–3pm and 7pm–midnight, 9 rue Moulay Ali Chérif (tel: 76 88 85).*

Le Fouquet's DD
Good European and Moroccan food in a small but cosy dining room. *285 avenue Mohammed V (tel: 76 80 07).*

MARRAKECH AND HIGH ATLAS

ESSAOUIRA
Chez Sam DDD
A seafood institution, perched on the edge of the docks. *Port de Pêche (tel: 47 35 13).*

MARRAKECH
Glacier Afoud D
New town restaurant serving good value salads, omelettes and couscous. *33 avenue Mohammed V (tel: 44 88 97).*

Jemaa el Fna D
Nothing compares with a grilled meal on a wood bench in the heart of the chaotic Jemaa (see page 90).

Le Jacaranda DD
Fine French cooking using local specialities. *32 boulevard Mohammed-Zerktouni (tel: 44 72 15).*

Marrakech L'Imperiale DDDD
The showcase of the Hotel Mamounia – evening dress required for a banquet at the height of luxury. *Hotel Mamounia, avenue Bab Jdid (tel: 44 89 81).*

Restaurant Yacout DDDD
Restored médina palace, on various

floors. *Sidi Ahmed Soussi, east of Jemaa el Fna (tel: 44 01 23).*

THE SOUTH

AGADIR
La Miramar DD
Italian restaurant specialising in sea food. *Boulevard Mohammed V (tel: 84 07 70).*

La Pergola DD
Rustic French restaurant. *Inezgane, 8km Route d'Agadir (tel: 83 08 41).*

OUARZAZATE
Chez Dimitri DD
Opened in 1928 to serve the French Foreign legion, Dimitri's is a Ouarzazate institution, offering French and Italian fare. *Avenue Mohammed V.*

Kasbah de Tifoultoute DD
The old kasbah became a hotel when Lawrence of Arabia was filmed here. Excellent Moroccan food, often with a folk spectacle in the evening. *8km northwest of centre (tel: 88 28 13).*

TAROUDANNT
Taroudannt Hotel D
Good French and Moroccan cuisine. *Place Assarag (tel: 85 24 16).*

CAFÉS

CASABLANCA
Oliveri
Late-night coffee and ice cream. *132 avenue Hassan II (tel: 27 60 75).*

ESSAOUIRA
Pâtisserie Driss
Orange juice, coffee and fresh croissants amid the fishermen and surfers of Essaouira. *10 rue Hajjali.*

MARRAKECH
Café Glacier and Café de la Place
Overlooking the Jemaa el Fna. The Café de France is more crowded and has less of a view. *East side of the Jemaa el Fna.*

Café Renaissance
A lift takes you to the 9th floor and a view over Marrakech up to the High Atlas. *Avenue Mohammed V, Gueliz.*

RABAT
Café des Maures
Through the Andalusian garden of the kasbah, overlooking the estuary. *Kasbah des Oudayas.*

TANGER
Café de France
A favourite of Paul Bowles and William S Burroughs; the hub of Tanger. *Place de France (tel: 93 84 44).*

Café de Paris
A legacy of the colonial occupation. *Place de France.*

Café Central
The place of a thousand illicit deals. Unmissable. *Petit Socco.*

The eternally popular Café de Paris in Tanger

TEA

Mint tea is the life-blood of Morocco and you will be offered it wherever you go. More than mere refreshment, more than mere social lubrication, a glass of mint tea is an avowal of friendship, and should not be rejected at any time. It is drunk day and night, often in vast quantities. Green Chinese tea is used, originally introduced by British traders in the 1800s. The mint is Moroccan, the best variety coming from Meknès. The tea is always very sweet, with plenty of sugar.

Apart from its culinary role as a refreshing summer drink and a warming winter tipple, mint tea is also highly symbolic. The green of the tea is also the green of the Prophet Mohammed, and thus brings great good luck.

Green is also the colour of fertility, the most prestigious of Moroccan blessings. The high sugar content is a token of sweet friendship and a blessing for continuous good health.

Attending a tea ceremony is one of the classic pleasures of visiting Morocco. The ceremony is ancient and learned by the young from an early age. An honoured guest is chosen to make the tea, and sits cross-legged while a tray is set before him (honoured guests are usually male). On the tray are a silver teapot, small glasses and three boxes of tea, mint and sugar. In awed silence, a pinch of tea is put in the teapot and boiling water added, followed by sugar and fresh mint. The teapot is then left to infuse. The guest eventually pours a taste for himself, which he swirls dramatically around his mouth; if satisfied, he pours for the others, always from a great height to ensure the tea is well mixed and that his presentation is amply appreciated. Guests must then drink at least three glasses for the host to be sure they have accepted his hospitality.

The Moroccan tea ceremony is a complex custom but a simple pleasure

Hotels and Accommodation

Morocco has always greeted visitors with warm hospitality, from the spice and gold traders of past centuries to the holidaymaker and business traveller of today. Cities like Casablanca, Fès and Marrakech contain numerous high-quality luxury hotels – indeed, the Mamounia in Marrakech is often cited as one of the top hotels in the world.

The Beach Club Hotel at Agadir

Most Moroccan towns offer two distinct hotel districts: the médina and the new town (Ville Nouvelle). Médina hotels, whilst close to the action and immersed in local life, are mostly unclassified and offer reduced security. Most visitors stay in new town classified hotels, enjoying modern, safe accommodation.

The north of Morocco is busiest in summer, and reservations are recommended. Mountain resorts are also busy, particularly in the Middle Atlas. Further south, high season tends to be from October to April, especially around Marrakech and down to Ouarzazate. Christmas and Easter are busy throughout Morocco and it is advisable to book in advance.

Standards of service and hygiene are generally good, although in small towns and villages facilities are naturally more limited. Many down-market hotels have private bathroom facilities in each room, although it is rare to find a plug, due to the Muslim tradition of washing under running water. There have been recent water shortages in some parts of Morocco – use water conscientiously.

CATEGORIES AND PRICES

Each classification has A and B ratings, which vary slightly in amenities and price.

5-star 600DH–2,300DH per night
4-star A+B: 350DH–700DH
3-star A+B: 250DH–400DH
2-star A+B: 150DH–300DH
1-star A+B: 70DH–200DH

Travellers who purchase their travel tickets from a Thomas Cook network location are entitled to use the services of any other Thomas Cook network location, free of charge, to make hotel reservations.

DOS AND DON'TS

Room prices should include a 17–19 per cent tax, and be posted at hotel reception. Prices indicated are maximum prices for the hotel in the particular category. Off-season it may be possible to get special rates. For four- and five-star hotels it is advisable to book in advance, as these establishments rely on tour groups and may be reluctant to accept individual travellers on the spot. The ONMT tourist office in each town will be able to help with hotel reservations.

It is unwise to drink tap water (most up-market hotels supply mineral water), and therefore ice cubes should be avoided too. Many modern hotels now rely on solar power for hot water heating, and consequently supplies of hot water in the evening are not infinite. Tipping is only expected in five-star hotels – 10DH is sufficient.

HOTELS PALAIS

If you have ever dreamed of sleeping in a palace, Morocco is the place to do it. A handful of opulent palaces have been converted into some of the world's most luxurious hotels, the Hotels Palais. Of these the most famous is the **Hotel Palais Jamaï** in Fès, the 19th-century residence of the Jamaï family, viziers to Sultan Moulay Hassan. The hotel boasts some magnificent suites with views over the médina, although the new block is disappointing. Morocco's top hotel, one of the top three in the world, is the **Mamounia** in Marrakech. Once an Alaouite palace, the newly refurbished Mamounia was a favourite of Winston Churchill and offers the last word in luxury. Further south, near Taroudannt, the **Gazelle d'Or** was once home to a French baron, with views up to the High Atlas – its grass is still cut by hand. In Taroudannt itself, **Hotel Palais Salam** is an 18th-century palace built into the town's medieval walls. In keeping with this luxurious tradition, two new hotels have been built according to the lavish standards of the Hotels Palais – the **Jnan Palace** in Fès, and the **Palmeraie Golf Palace** in Marrakech, both of which offer sumptuous surroundings and excellent service.

Attentive service on the patio of the Jnan Palace in Fès

Breakfast in splendour at the Royal Mansour in Casablanca

Jnan Palace in Fès or the **Royal Mansour** in Casablanca offer all mod-cons – fine restaurants, discotheques, cocktail bars, 24-hour room service and business facilities such as faxing, secretarial services and conference rooms. Prices compare favourably with equivalent accommodation in Europe and North America. Four-star hotels are plentiful and offer high standards of service and cleanliness without the luxury of five-star accommodation. Older hotels such as **Hotel Rif** in Meknès have a characterful 'period' feel, while modern seaside hotels such as **Hotel Solazur** in Tanger or the delightful **Hotel Kabila** at M'Diq have been built specifically for the package holiday market, with all the expected facilities.

Standard accommodation

Mid-range accommodation varies considerably, but still maintains good standards at inexpensive prices. Many three-star hotels offer swimming pools. Much standard accommodation dates from the French occupation, and retains a certain venerable charm. **Hotel Balima**, in Rabat, was the first purpose-built hotel in Morocco, completed in 1932, with huge rooms and fading red upholstery.

Budget accommodation

Morocco has no lack of budget accommodation. Most is found in the médinas of Moroccan towns. Here, you are close to the action and able to participate in everyday Moroccan life; conversely, you are in a confusing maze of streets, often faced with lower standard rooms and plumbing, and

WHERE TO STAY

To get the most out of your holiday try to mix your accommodation, spending some nights in cheaper places and splashing out on top-class hotels when the occasion arises. Morocco is one of the few countries where you can alternate between the two ends of the hotel market and still enjoy a warm welcome and authentic accommodation.

Four- and five-star accommodation

Morocco's top-quality accommodation rivals any in the world. Hotels like the

FAMILY HOTELS

Another relic of French occupation in Morocco is the scattering of small family-run hotels, similar to French country *auberges*. Usually found in rural areas, especially the Middle and High Atlas, they are inexpensive, sometimes rudimentary but always welcoming. Many are preserved much as they were during the French Protectorate, with red checked table cloths, fine wine cellars and stuffed animals over the bar. Of these the most enchanting are the **Chalet du Lac**, on the shores of Dayet Aowa in the Middle Atlas, the **Sanglier qui Fume**, at Ouirgane, and **Auberge du Lac**, bordering Bin el Ouidane reservoir in the High Atlas. A more modern approach is found at **Villa Maroc**, in Essaouira, a renovated former brothel run by an English couple.

The sun-filled rooftops of the Villa Maroc in Essaouira

cannot guarantee the security of your belongings. At best médina hotels are cheap, immaculate, with white-washed rooms around a central airy courtyard. Such paradise is more likely to be found in smaller towns: **Casa Hassan** in the middle of Chechaouen's médina and **Hotel des Remparts** in Essaouira are good examples of médina accommodation at its best. Outside the médina, one- and two-star hotels are more secure and more likely to enjoy running water.

Young families

Along the Mediterranean and Atlantic coasts, some of the best value accommodation is to be found in tourist villages. These complexes offer small apartment accommodation around central shared facilities such as swimming pools, tennis courts, playgrounds and restaurants and are ideal for young families. On the Mediterranean coast, resorts such as **Kabila**, **Cabo Negro** and the newly built **MarinaSmir** are havens for those with young children – safe, attractively designed, close to the sea and inexpensive. On the Atlantic coast, Agadir has no fewer than 30 such 'villages' to suit all tastes and pockets.

On Business

BANKS

Banking has been restructured, but remains highly regulated. Moroccan banks operate under one of the toughest lending limits in the world: 7 per cent of net capital funds per borrower, compared with 25 per cent elsewhere. When setting up a company in Morocco it is necessary to open a Moroccan bank account, where at least a quarter of the capital investment should be deposited.

Firm state control over Moroccan banking is gradually being relaxed

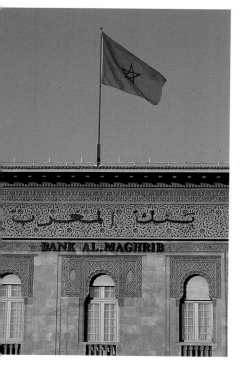

BUSINESS HOURS

Most times in Morocco are counted using the 24 hour clock.

Banks

(Winter) Monday to Friday, 8.30am–11.30am and 2.15pm–4.30pm. (Summer and Ramadan) Monday to Friday, 8.30am– 2pm.

Business offices

(Winter) Monday to Friday, 9am–noon and 3pm–6pm. (Summer) Monday to Friday, 8am–2.30pm.

Government offices

(Winter) Monday to Friday, 8.30am–noon and 2.30pm–6pm. Saturday, 8.30am–1pm. (Summer) Monday to Saturday, 8am– 2pm.

CAPITAL INVESTMENT

Foreigners may invest foreign capital in Morocco as hard currency, tangible fixed assets (eg machinery, tools) or intangible fixed assets (eg patents, trademarks). Transfer of the capital invested, any income generated by that capital and any capital gains realised is permitted.

CHAMBERS OF COMMERCE

Moroccan Chamber of Commerce, Grand Casablanca Chamber of Commerce, 98 boulevard Mohammed V, Casablanca (tel: 30 99 66/30 06 75).
The British Chamber of Commerce for Morocco, Suite 201, Holiday Inn, Crowne Plaza, Rond Point Hassan II, Casablanca (tel: 27 15 19).

CONFERENCE FACILITIES

In Casablanca the largest conference facilities are provided by the **Royal Mansour** *27 avenue des FAR (tel: 31 30 11, fax: 31 25 83).* In Fès the new **Jnan**

Palace offers a 1,300-person capacity: *avenue Ahmed Chaouki (tel: 65 39 65, fax: 65 19 17)*. In Marrakech the vast **Palmeraie Golf Palace** combines a 1,200-person conference capacity with an 18-hole golf course: *Les Jardins de la Palmeraie (tel: 30 10 10, fax 30 20 20)*. Also in Marrakech, the **Palais des Congrès de Marrakech** can provide 16 fully equipped conference rooms with 25- to 2,800-person capacity.

ETIQUETTE
Remember that Morocco is a Muslim state. It is best not to schedule business meetings for Friday, the day of prayer. Alcohol and smoking are not permitted for Muslims during Ramadan.

EXCHANGE RATE
In January 1993 the Dirham was made convertible for all transactions on current account by foreign investors and Moroccan residents abroad. This makes it much easier to transfer investment funds in and out of the country. Otherwise the Moroccan Dirham is not freely convertible, and cannot be exchanged outside Morocco. Rates are fixed by the Moroccan Government.

EXHIBITION ORGANISERS
Casablanca:
KTI, *4 rue des Hirondelles, Rond Point Racine (tel: (02) 39 85 72, fax: 39 85 67)*.
Atlas Voyages, *44 avenue des FAR (tel: (02) 31 80 71, fax: 31 80 98)*.
Archoun Tourisme, *9 Gihali Ahmed (tel: (02) 27 11 42, fax: 27 55 00)*.

GOVERNMENT AGENCIES
Two important government agencies promoting business growth in Morocco are the **Office for Industrial Development** *10 Zenkat Gandhi, Rabat*

(tel: 72 21 81), and the **Centre Marocain de Promotion des Exportations** *23 boulevard Bnou Majed El-Bahar, Casablanca (tel: 30 22 10)*.

LANGUAGE
The main language of business is still French, with English a close second. Trade documents are usually in French. With increased Spanish investment, Spanish is more widely spoken.

MEDIA
A new weekly economic and financial weekly, *L'Economiste*, provides balanced and reliable market information.

PREMISES
Any company wishing to be recognised by the Moroccan authorities must have an office in Morocco. Foreigners may buy property only with foreign currency, payable at the Banque du Maroc.

TAX
Foreign individuals, diplomats and officials of foreign agencies are exempt from income tax. Foreigners whose residence is in Morocco or who live in Morocco for more than six consecutive months must pay tax. Companies based in Morocco pay corporate tax (IS) and value added tax (TVA).

TRANSLATION SERVICES
Traductec: translation, interpreting, conference organisation *31 Résidence minaret, rue Amman/Yougoslavie, Rabat (tel: 73 58 21, fax: 73 58 27)*.

WORK PERMITS
These are required by foreigners wishing to work in Morocco. Permission can be obtained from the Moroccan Embassy in your country.

Practical Guide

ARRIVING

Travellers from the UK, New Zealand, Australia, Canada and the USA do not require a visa for stays of 90 days or less. South African nationals require a visa. All categories of traveller must be in possession of a valid passport (British Visitor's Passports are not valid). Travellers who require visas should obtain them in their country of residence.

By air

Numerous international airlines fly to Morocco's main Mohammed V airport outside Casablanca. The most regular flights are available from Royal Air Maroc (RAM), the state airline, which also provides connections to all other Moroccan cities. RAM flies three times a week direct to Tanger and 6 times a week to Casablanca from London and from many other European cities. It offers one flight a week to Marrakech and one a week to Agadir, both via Casablanca. GB Airways flies via Gibraltar 3 times a week to Casablanca, once a week to Tanger and once a week to Marrakech.

From Mohammed V Airport an efficient train service leaves every 20 minutes to Casablanca and Rabat. Taxis take 30 minutes.

By car

The car ferry between Algeciras in Spain and Tanger runs 4 times a day, 6 times daily in summer, taking 2–3 hours. The other popular crossing is Algeciras to the Ceuta, with up to 10 departures during high season, taking 1½ hours.

By rail

Sleepers depart daily from Paris to
Madrid (13 hours), where passengers
must change trains for Algeciras (11
hours). The *Thomas Cook Overseas
Timetable* gives details of many rail, bus
and shipping services worldwide, and will
help you plan a rail journey to, from and
around Morocco. It is available in the
UK from some stations, any branch of
Thomas Cook, or by phoning 01733
268943. In the USA, contact the Forsyth
Travel Library Inc. *9154 West 57th St
(PO Box 2975), Shawnee Mission, Kansas
66201, tel: (800) 367 7982 (toll-free)*.

CAMPING

Camping is widespread in Morocco.
Sixty-eight campsites are officially
recognised by the Tourist Office, the
majority offering adequate shower and
toilet facilities, food and electricity for
caravans. Camping in Arabic is
moukhayyem.

WEATHER CONVERSION CHART
25.4mm = 1 inch
°F = 1.8 × °C + 32

CLIMATE

The northern half of the country has two
distinct seasons: winter is wet and mild
along the coast and cold and icy in the
mountains, with temperatures falling
below freezing. Summer is hot and
sunny.

In the south it is either hot or hotter
with temperatures rising to 45°C (nights
can get cool in winter months).

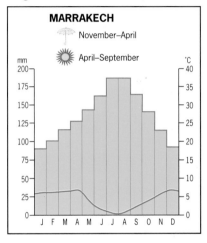

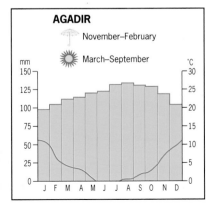

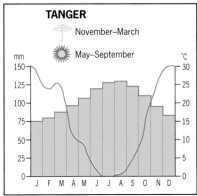

CRIME

Violent crime rates are very low. Petty thefts are, however, commonplace – take sensible precautions, especially in the big cities. Carry only small amounts of cash and use a money belt for passports and valuables. For Thomas Cook Travellers' cheque loss or theft contact the emergency telephone number on page 182.

When driving, do not leave luggage and valuables accessible in the car. Most horror stories involve drug transactions – the police are less than sympathetic for a tourist threatened over a drug deal.

CUSTOMS REGULATIONS

On entry, duty-free limits are 200 cigarettes, 1 bottle of wine, 1 bottle of spirits, 25cl of perfume. The import of all narcotics is forbidden and carries stiff prison sentences. There is no restriction on the import of foreign currency but the Moroccan dirham cannot be imported or exported.

DISABLED TRAVELLERS

There are few specially adapted facilities for disabled travellers. Most moderate–expensive hotels have lift services and some, like the Jnan Palace in Fès, have installed wheelchair ramps throughout. Wheelchairs are available at all international airports. The Moroccan National Tourist Office can provide information on your destination prior to departure.

DRIVING
Car hire

Car hire is expensive in Morocco. Often it is cheaper to arrange a deal from home, paying in your local currency. All the main international companies have representatives in Morocco: of these one is the most reliable with offices in every town in Morocco is **Europcar** *44 avenue des FAR Casablanca (tel: 31 37 37, fax: 31 03 60)*.

Budget, Avis and Hertz all have offices in Morocco. Local companies sometimes offer better deals. **Stopcars** in Fès and Meknès offer interesting weekend rates: *7 rue Larbi Karrat, boulevard Mohammed V (tel: 62 08 67)*.

To hire a car you must be over 21 and possess a full driver's licence. Always check that the spare tyre is in good condition, and try the brakes if possible. The only legally required insurance is third party, but it is advisable to take out the extra Collision Damage Waiver and Personal Accident insurance to cover all eventualities.

Emergency

In the event of an emergency contact the nearest police post. You will find police road checks every 70km or so – these are standard throughout Morocco, and you will be asked for your driving papers.

Insurance

If you are bringing a car from Europe make sure your insurance includes a Green Card covering Morocco. If it does not you will be able to buy insurance on arriving at frontier posts; apart from Green Cards, insurance policies are not valid unless issued by a company with an office in Morocco. The Moroccan Insurance Bureau is **Bureau Central Marocain d'Assurances** *100 rue Mostafa el Manni, Casablanca*.

Parking

Everywhere you stop, someone will appear offering to 'guard' your vehicle. These attendants are the Moroccan equivalent of the parking meter and a

The trusty Renault 4, Morocco's most popular rental car

vital part of the local economy; 2 dirhams is a usual fee for daytime parking, 5 dirhams for overnight.

Petrol

Petrol is widely available in four-star and diesel forms. Unleaded is becoming more common, with 65 petrol stations now offering 'green' fuel. In remote areas, especially in the south, fill up whenever possible.

Roads

Morocco boasts the most extensive motoring network in North Africa, with 56,000km of roads, 25,000km of which are asphalt. In winter some mountain passes may be blocked by snow. In spring beware of flash floods in river valleys, especially in the High Atlas and the south. Further information is available from the **Touring Club of Morocco**, *3 avenue de l'Armée Royale, Casablanca (tel: 27 13 04)*.

Speed Limits

Limits are 100km an hour outside towns, 40km an hour within town limits.

DRUGS

Historically, most of the marijuana exported to Europe originated in Morocco. However, in recent years the authorities have been cracking down on the cultivation and trafficking of the drug and those caught in possession face prison sentences. Do not, under any circumstances, accept packages from strangers, and avoid the kif-growing areas of the Rif.

ELECTRICITY
Most installations are 220V, but in smaller towns 110V may still be in use. Sockets take European style round two-pin plugs.

EMBASSIES AND CONSULATES
Australia: c/o UK
Canada: Rabat Embassy *13 Joafar Essadik Agday (tel: 77 13 75)*.
New Zealand: c/o UK
Republic of Ireland: c/o UK
UK: Casablanca Consulate, *60 boulevard d'Anfa (tel: 22 16 53)*. Rabat Embassy, *17 boulevard de la Tour Hassan (tel: 72 09 05)*. Tanger Consulate, *9 rue d'Amerique du Sud (tel: 93 58 95)*.
US: Casablanca Consulate, *8 boulvard Moulay Youssef (tel: 22 41 49)*. Rabat Embassy, *2 avenue de Marrakech (tel: 76 22 65)*.

EMERGENCY TELEPHONE NUMBERS
Police 19
Fire service/Ambulance 15

The Thomas Cook Worldwide Customer Promise offers free emergency assistance at any Thomas Cook Network location to travellers who have purchased their travel tickets at a Thomas Cook location.

In addition, MasterCard cardholders may use any Thomas Cook Network location to report loss or theft of their card and obtain an emergency card replacement, as a free service under the Thomas Cook MasterCard International Alliance. Thomas Cook travellers' cheque refund (24-hour service – report loss or theft within 24 hours): +44 733 502 995.

HEALTH AND INSURANCE
Up-to-date health advice can be obtained from your Thomas Cook travel consultant. There are no mandatory vaccination requirements, and no vaccination recommendations other than to keep tetanus and polio immunisation up to date. Like every other part of the world, AIDS is present. Medical insurance is advisable for travel to Morocco, as part of a travel insurance package.

Strict food and water hygiene is essential to avoid problems with diarrhoea. Make sure food has been properly prepared; drink boiled or bottled water only, and remember that ice cubes will have been made with tap water. In the south, do not bathe in rivers, as bilharzia is prevelant.

Pharmacies are widespread and well-stocked with most European medicines. Most pharmacists speak French, although local Tourist Offices will be able to direct you to an English-speaking chemist.

HITCH-HIKING
Hitch-hiking is possible in rural areas but is not recommended. In areas where bus services are infrequent locals will pay the equivalent of a bus ticket for a ride in a private vehicle – you will be expected to do the same. Never hitch-hike alone.

LANGUAGE

Morocco's first language is Arabic, although up to 40 per cent of the population speak Berber dialects. French is widely spoken, and many Moroccans are bilingual Arabic-French.

Arabic

While it is impossible to learn Moroccan Arabic over a short stay, employing a few key phrases will impress and amuse your hosts, and may aid the bargaining process in souks. Most Moroccans speak some French. The American Institute in Fès runs regular language courses: *PO Box 2136, Fès. Tel/fax: 212 5 62 48 50.*

Pronunciation

There are no silent letters – pronounce all that is written.
kh = ch (like Scottish loch) as in *Msa l'khir* = Msa l'chir
gh = like the French rolling 'r' as in *gheda* = rreda
ai = like 'eye' as in *baggai* = bageye
q = like k as in *qreeb* = kreeb
j = like s in 'sure' as in *joob* = soob

Numbers

Arabic numbers are based on symbols 1-9.

1 *wahèd*	**10** *achra*
2 *jooj*	**20** *chrin*
3 *tlàta*	**50** *khamsin*
4 *àrba*	**1,000** *alef*
5 *khàmsa*	
6 *sètta*	
7 *sèba*	
8 *tmènia*	
9 *tseud*	

Everyday expressions

Hello (informal)	*La bes*
Hello (more formal)	*Salamalaykoom*
Goodbye	*beslamah*
Good morning	*sbah el khir*
Good afternoon	*msa el khir*
Good night *leela*	*saieeda*
Please	*minfadlik*
Thank you	*choukrane*
Yes/no	*wakha/la*
Where is?	*fayn kayn?*
How much?	*bsh hal?*
Too expensive	*ghalee bzef*
Cheaper	*rkhiss*
Okay	*wakha*
Big	*kebir*
Small	*seghir*
Go away	*emshee*
Today	*elyoum*
Yesterday	*elbarah*
Tomorrow	*ghedda*

Days of the week

Sunday	*nhar el had*
Monday	*nhar el tnin*
Tuesday	*nahr el tlata*
Wednesday	*nhar el arba*
Thursday	*nhar el khemis*
Friday	*el jmaa*
Saturday	*nhat es Sebt*

MAPS

The most widely available and inclusive road map of Morocco is the red Michelin number 969. More detailed maps of hiking are available in many bookshops, and at Imlil, departure point for the Mount Toubkal ascent.

MEASUREMENTS AND SIZES

See opposite.

MEDIA

British and French newspapers are available in big cities. The *International Herald Tribune* is also easy to find. Local

The sand dunes of Diabat

Men's Suits

UK	36	38	40	42	44	46	48
Rest of Europe	46	48	50	52	54	56	58
US	36	38	40	42	44	46	48

Dress Sizes

UK	8	10	12	14	16	18
France	36	38	40	42	44	46
Italy	38	40	42	44	46	48
Rest of Europe	34	36	38	40	42	44
US	6	8	10	12	14	16

Men's Shirts

UK	14	14.5	15	15.5	16	16.5	17
Rest of Europe	36	37	38	39/40	41	42	43
US	14	14.5	15	15.5	16	16.5	17

Men's Shoes

UK	7	7.5	8.5	9.5	10.5	11
Rest of Europe	41	42	43	44	45	46
US	8	8.5	9.5	10.5	11.5	12

Women's Shoes

UK	4.5	5	5.5	6	6.5	7
Rest of Europe	38	38	39	39	40	41
US	6	6.5	7	7.5	8	8.5

Conversion Table

FROM	TO	MULTIPLY BY
Inches	Centimetres	2.54
Feet	Metres	0.3048
Yards	Metres	0.9144
Miles	Kilometres	1.6090
Acres	Hectares	0.4047
Gallons	Litres	4.5460
Ounces	Grams	28.35
Pounds	Grams	453.6
Pounds	Kilograms	0.4536
Tons	Tonnes	1.0160

To convert back, for example from centimetres to inches, divide by the number in the the third column.

press is divided between French and Arabic dailies. The main French papers are the pro-government _Le Matin Du Sahara_, the opposition _L'Opinion_ and the communist _Al-Bayanne_. Of the Arabic papers, _Al-Alam_, loyal to the Istiqlal party, has the widest circulation.

BBC World service is theoretically found on short wave 15.07 mHz and 17.705 mHz. Most large hotels have satellite TV, receiving CNN news and European Sky news. Moroccan television broadcasts many programmes in French.

MONEY MATTERS

The Moroccan dirham is not exchangeable outside Morocco. It is illegal to import or export Moroccan dirhams. When nearing the end of your stay it is wise to shed as many of your dirhams as possible, budgeting carefully. To exchange dirhams on leaving Morocco you must show your exchange receipts – you can change back 50 per cent of the sums totalled on your receipts.

Most small towns have banks at which you can change travellers'

cheques. The rate is fixed by the government and there is little competition between banks. Big hotels also change travellers' cheques at rates similar to, if not better than banks. Credit cards are taken in most large hotels and up-market restaurants; Visa is the most widely accepted.

Thomas Cook MasterCard travellers' cheques can quickly be refunded in the event of loss or theft (see emergency telephone number, page 182, and emergency help locations below). US Dollar, Sterling, Deutsche Mark, French and Swiss Franc travellers' cheques are all accepted. Major hotels and some restaurants and shops in main tourist and commercial areas accept travellers' cheques in lieu of cash.

The following branch of Thomas Cook can provide emergency assistance in the case of loss or theft of Thomas Cook MasterCard travellers' cheques: **KTI Voyages** _4 rue des Hirondelles, Rond Point Racine, Casablanca (tel: 39 85 72, fax: 39 85 67)._

A Moroccan 50 Dirham note

Religious Holidays

The main religious festival is that of Ramadan (see page 25). The dates for religious festivals follow the lunar calendar and therefore move backwards by 11 days each year. Approximate dates are as follows:

	1994	1995	1996
Ramadan	11 Feb–10 Mar	31 Jan–1 Mar	21 Jan–20 Feb
Aid El-Fitr	11–12 Mar	2–3 Mar	21–22 Feb
Aid Al-Adha	20–21 May	11–12 May	2–3 May
Muslim New Year	10–11 Jun	1–2 Jun	23–24 Jun
Achoura	19–20 Jun	10–11 Jun	1–2 Jul
Prophet's Birthday	19–20 Aug	10–11 Aug	1–2 Aug

NATIONAL HOLIDAYS

Official Holidays
1 January New Year's Day
11 January Manifesto of Independence
3 March Feast of the Throne
1 May Labour Day
23 May National Feast
9 July Youth Day (King's Birthday)
14 August Allegiance of Oued Ed-Dahab
6 November Green March Anniversary
18 November Independence Day

OPENING HOURS
Banks
(Winter) Monday to Friday 8.30am–11.30am and 2.15pm–4.30pm. (Summer and Ramadan) Monday to Friday 8.30am–2pm.
Shops
Weekly 9am–8pm (in practice most close for lunch).
Museums
Weekly 8.30am–noon and 3pm–6pm.
Government offices
(Winter) Monday to Friday 8.30am–noon and 2.30pm–6pm. Saturday 8.30–1pm. (Summer) Monday to Saturday 8am–2pm.

ORGANISED TOURS
Thomas Cook can handle bookings for all major Moroccan operators.

PHOTOGRAPHY
Film is widely available, at comparable prices to European countries. For photographs in towns, especially in médinas, where there is contrast between light and shade, fast film is useful – 400 ASA. Slower film is better for landscape shots.

Always ask before taking someone's picture, and never insist. Street entertainers expect payment for a picture (they are, after all, putting on a professional show). Do not give money to children to take their pictures – they will prefer modelling to schooling.

PLACES OF WORSHIP
St Andrew's English Church in Tanger is the only Anglican church in Morocco and has weekly services. Otherwise there are numerous Catholic churches, even in many of the smaller towns. The main synagogue is in Casablanca, with smaller ones in Tanger and Marrakech.

Islamic beliefs are understandably well catered for.

POLICE

There are two types of police in Morocco – the *gendarmerie*, dressed in khaki with green berets, and the *sureté nationale*, who wear grey. The *gendarmerie* deal more with internal security, while the *sureté nationale* carry out local policing in towns and are responsible for tourists. The police emergency telephone number is 19.

POST OFFICES

Moroccan post offices demand perseverance and resilience. With 2 million Moroccans working abroad, postal communications are stretched to their limits – queues are part of the experience. Letters take about a week to get to Europe, two to North America and Australasia. Stamps are more rapidly purchased in tourist shops and hotels. Post offices are open Monday to Friday 8.30am–noon and 3pm–6pm in winter and 8am–3pm in summer.

PUBLIC TRANSPORT

Air

Royal Air Maroc serves most major towns within Morocco and has offices throughout the country. Flying is relatively inexpensive and is highly

A Surêté policeman

recommended to cover long distances (Tanger–Marrakech and particularly to the Deep South and La'youne). RAM has ticket reservation offices in all major cities in the country. The main offices are: Agadir, avenue Général Kettani (tel: 84 07 93), Casablanca, 44 avenue des Forces Armées Royales (tel: 31 11 22), Marrakech, 197 avenue Mohammed V (tel: 43 62 05) and Tanger, place de France (tel: 93 55 01).

Buses

Bus services between towns are often full and it is necessary to reserve in advance. The two main companies are the national carrier CTM and the private SATAS. Costs are marginally cheaper than *grands taxis*, but journeys take much longer. There are numerous small private outfits, all of which will approach you at bus stations: these are far from reliable and it is best to stick to the main carriers.

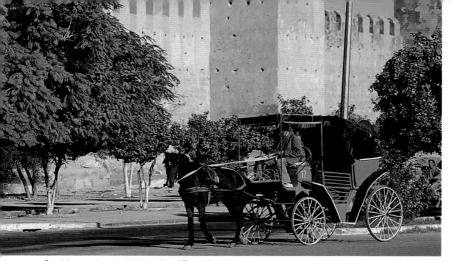

Catching a cab around the walls of Taroudannt

Taxis

Within towns *petits taxis* are cheap and efficient. By law fares should be determined by a meter – insist on the *compteur* being turned on. A battle of will might ensue, but always remember the law is on your side. After 10pm the driver can add 50 per cent to the metered fare.

Routes between towns are served by *grands taxis*: usually large, antiquated Mercedes. These depart from designated taxi stations, and have the advantage of being quicker than buses and not bound to timetables. You pay a fixed rate per place in the car, which will leave only when it is full (usually six passengers). If you want to leave before the driver has found six passengers you must pay for the empty places.

Trains

Trains are efficient and fairly comfortable in Morocco, but offer a limited number of routes. For longer journeys it may be preferable to pay a little extra for a first-class seat, as these are more spacious and comfortable. Most stations are conveniently situated in the new quarters of Moroccan towns, close to hotels. Only a few have left luggage offices – hotels and even cafés may lock up bags for a small fee.

STUDENT AND YOUTH TRAVEL

The International Student Card is largely redundant in Morocco - there are no student reductions on museum and site entry. RAM offers 25 per cent discount on internal flights to students when tickets are bought in advance, and ONCF offer 50 per cent discounts on a package of more than eight return train trips within Morocco. European Interail passes extend to the Moroccan rail system.

TELEPHONES AND FAXES

All big hotels can fax for you, although charges are much higher than in Europe and North America. There are also shops which specialise in faxing, although these are often more expensive than hotels.

There are two ways to make a telephone call from Morocco. The first is at the Post Office, where you make a direct call in a designated telephone cubicle. Once the call is finished you pay for the units used at a central desk. There are now also phones which take telephone cards – these are found outside Post Offices. Cards are sold in local shops and by legions of young men who hang around the phones.

The second possibility is to call from your hotel – much easier, but three times the cost of calling from the Post Office.

For local calls dial the area code then the number. For international calls dial 00 and the country code and the number. The country code for the UK is 44, Ireland is 353, USA and Canada is 1, Australia is 61 and New Zealand is 64. Within Morocco important numbers are:

16 Directory enquiries
10 Operator
12 International operator

Main local codes are as follows: Agadir and region – 08, Casablanca – 02, El Jadida – 03, Fès and region – 05, Marrakech and region – 04, Mohammedia – 03, Oujda and region – 06, Rabat – 07, Tanger and region – 09.

TIME

Morocco follows Greenwich Mean Time all year.

TIPPING

You will be expected to tip frequently in Morocco. Always carry a pocket of small change to pay parking attendants, guides and waiters. Even if a service charge is included in your bill it is customary to pay an extra 7–10 per cent to the waiter. In big hotels valets expect 10 dirhams for their services.

Islam encourages the giving of alms (*zakat*) and most Moroccans give generously to beggars in the street. An offering of a few coins (a paltry sum in Western terms) is a customary gesture.

TOILETS

Moroccan toilets do not have the best reputation in the world. Where tourists congregate they are comparable with Western toilets; elsewhere things are little more than rudimentary. It is wise to carry a roll of toilet paper. Courage is of the essence.

TOURIST OFFICES

Each Moroccan town has its tourist office, the ONMT. Several towns also possess Syndicats d'Initiatives, which provide similar facilities. The main tourist offices are as follow:

Agadir *place Heritier Sidi Mohammed. Tel: 82 28 94.*

Casablanca *55 rue Omar Slaoui. Tel: 27 17 77, fax: 20 59 29.*

Fès *place de la Résistance. Tel: 62 34 60.*

Marrakech *place Abdelmoumen Ben Ali. Tel: 44 88 89, fax: 44 89 06.*

Meknès *place Administrative. Tel: 52 44 26.*

Ouarzazate *avenue Mohammed V. Tel: 88 24 85.*

Rabat *22 avenue d'Alger. Tel: 73 05 62.*

Tanger *29 boulevard Pasteur. Tel: 93 82 39.*

Tetouan *30 avenue Mohammed V. Tel: 96 44 07.*

The tourist office on boulevard Pasteur, Tanger

ACKNOWLEDGEMENTS
The Automobile Association wishes to thank the following photographers and libraries for their assistance in the preparation of this book.

MARY EVANS PICTURE LIBRARY 11b, 39a, 39b
MOROCCAN TOURIST OFFICE, LONDON 28, 31, 92, 134, 140, 156, 157
REX FEATURES LTD 20

The remaining photographs are held in the Automobile Association's own photo library (AA PHOTO LIBRARY) and were taken by Ian Burgum with the exception of the cover, inset and spine pictures, and pages 1, 2, 5, 8, 12, 15, 16a, 27, 29, 37, 53, 58, 60a, 60c, 81, 83, 91a, 91b, 93, 118, 124, 125a, 125b, 132b, 135, 137a, 153, 163, 168, 170, 182, 188 which were taken by Paul Kenward.

The photographer would like to thank the following for their assistance: Mrs Leila Boubia of the Moroccan Tourist Office, London; The American Legation in Tanger for their permission to take photographs and GB Airways.

The author would like to thank Royal Air Maroc for their kind assistance.

The Automobile Association would also like to thank Jean Celeste, Secretary General of the Touring Club du Maroc, and the Moroccan National Tourist Office for their invaluable help in ensuring the accuracy of the information in the book

CONTRIBUTORS
Series adviser: Melissa Shales   **Designer:** Design 23   **Copy editor:** Nia Williams
Verifier: Judy Sykes   **Indexer:** Marie Lorimer